INTERNATIONAL COMPETITION IN SERVICES

INTERNATIONAL COMPETITION IN SERVICES

A Constitutional Framework

John H. Jackson

COMPETING IN A
CHANGING WORLD ECONOMY
PROJECT

American Enterprise Institute for Public Policy Research
Washington, D.C.

338
.6048
J13i

Distributed by arrangement with

UPA, Inc.
4720 Boston Way   3 Henrietta Street
Lanham, Md. 20706   London WC2E 8LU England

Library of Congress Cataloging-in-Publication Data

Jackson, John Howard, 1932–
  International competition in services : a constitutional framework
/ John H. Jackson.
    p. cm. — (AEI studies ; 478)
    Includes index.
    ISBN 0-8447-3664-3 (alk. paper)
    1. Service industries—International cooperation.   2. Competition,
International.   3. Commercial treaties.   I. Title.   II. Series.
HD9980.6.J33   1988
338.6'048—dc19   88-16816
                                                                  CIP

1 3 5 7 9 10 8 6 4 2

AEI Studies 478

Printed in the United States of America

Contents

FOREWORD *Christopher C. DeMuth*   vii

ABOUT THE AUTHOR   ix

PART ONE
A CONSTITUTIONAL STRUCTURE FOR INTERNATIONAL
COOPERATION IN TRADE IN SERVICES
John H. Jackson

1 INTRODUCTION AND THE BASIC POLICY GOALS   3

Trade in Services and the World Economy   3
Trade in Goods: The GATT Structure Reviewed   7
Policy Goals for a Services Agreement   10

2 STRUCTURE OF A CONSTITUTION FOR SERVICES TRADE   15

Relation to the GATT   15
The Structure of a Constitution   17
Relation to U.S. Law and Other National Laws   18

3 POSSIBLE CONTENTS OF AN UMBRELLA AGREEMENT   20

Statement of Objectives   20
Institutional Measures   21
Dispute Settlement   23
Transparency Obligations   24
Regulatory Due Process   25
Relation to Sector Agreements   25
Most-Favored-Nation Provisions   26
National Treatment Obligation   28
General Exceptions   29
Waiver Provisions   30
Measures for Developing Countries   30
Reciprocity   31
Final Clauses   31
Existing International Service Agreements   31

4 THE OPTIONAL PROTOCOL AND SECTOR AGREEMENTS   34

   The Optional Protocol, or Middle Layer 34
   The Nature and Obligations of Sector
      Agreements 35

5 CONCLUSION   37

PART TWO
EVALUATION AND COMMENTARY

INTRODUCTORY COMMENTS   41
John S. Reed 41
Finn Caspersen 42

STATEMENT   43
John H. Jackson

COMMENTARY   48
Geza Feketekuty 48
Claude E. Barfield 53
Richard R. Rivers 55
Joan Spero 57

DISCUSSION   60

INDEX   67

Foreword

With the Uruguay round of trade negotiations now in full swing, negotiators, business people, scholars, and others must give serious consideration to the structure and details of a services agreement in the General Agreement on Tariffs and Trade (GATT). A wealth of information on trade in services has been generated in recent years. Recognizing the need to get to the heart of negotiating issues, the American Enterprise Institute commissioned a leading authority on the GATT, John H. Jackson, to analyze the issues surrounding a services agreement and to offer his recommendations for a draft agreement.

Mr. Jackson's paper was presented and discussed among government officials, business executives, and researchers at AEI's conference "Trade in Services: Open Markets and the Uruguay Round Negotiations," in Washington, D.C., in November 1987. This volume reproduces that paper as well as a portion of the debate that it sparked at the conference. Mr. Jackson's paper continues to stimulate discussions among U.S. trade officials and trade officials in other nations who are searching for a viable plan to bring services into the GATT.

The conference on trade in services and the Uruguay round negotiations was one of a series of conferences, seminars, publications, and special events developed under AEI's research project Competing in a Changing World Economy. The project is designed to examine basic structural changes in the world economy and to explore strategies for dealing with new economic, political, and strategic realities facing the United States.

CHRISTOPHER C. DEMUTH
President
American Enterprise Institute

About the Author

John H. Jackson, Hessel E. Yntema Professor of Law at the University of Michigan Law School, is a leading authority on the General Agreement on Tariffs and Trade (GATT). He received his A.B. degree from Princeton University and his J.D. and LL.B. degrees from the University of Michigan. In 1973–1974 he served as general counsel in the Office of the U.S. Special Trade Representative. Since then he has often served as a consultant to U.S. government agencies concerned with trade issues, including the U.S. Treasury, the Office of the U.S. Trade Representative, and the U.S. Senate Finance Committee. His numerous books and articles on the international trading system include *World Trade and the Law of GATT* (1969) and *Legal Problems of International Economic Relations* (1977).

Contributors

Claude E. Barfield, coordinator, Competing in a Changing World Economy, American Enterprise Institute

Finn Caspersen, chairman, Beneficial Finance Corporation; president, Coalition of Service Industries

Geza Feketekuty, counselor to the U.S. Trade Representative

John S. Reed, chairman, Citicorp; chairman, Coalition of Service Industries

Richard R. Rivers, partner, Akin, Gump, Strauss, Hauer & Feld

Joan Spero, senior vice president, international government affairs, American Express Company

PART ONE

A Constitutional Structure for International Cooperation in Trade in Services

John H. Jackson

1
Introduction and
the Basic Policy Goals

The need for international coordination and cooperation in services trade across borders has become apparent. Although a troubled and evolving international legal framework exists for trade in goods,[1] little of such a framework exists for services, except in certain sectors.[2] Services make up both a greater percentage of the gross national product of major industrial countries than production of goods and a significant percentage of world trade.[3]

Trade in Services and the World Economy

Services comprise an extremely broad set of economic activities, including banking, stockbrokerage, law, engineering, insurance, telecommunications, accounting, travel, tourism, the hotel industry, shipping, advertising, consulting, and construction. This varied range of activity is difficult to define, much less regulate.[4] Yet in many nations service activities are growing more rapidly than the production of goods. And in many nations (not necessarily the same ones) governments are increasingly tempted to step in and regulate those activities, often for legitimate reasons of protecting consumers or other national interests but also sometimes simply to protect local entrepreneurs from the rigors of competition from more efficient

The author wishes to acknowledge the assistance he has received from lengthy discussions with numerous individuals, including Geza Feketekuty and Richard Self of the Office of the U.S. Trade Representative, Professors Alan Deardorff and Robert Stern of the University of Michigan Economics Department, participants in the Trade in Services Project of the American Enterprise Institute, including the director, Claude Barfield, and Joan Spero of the American Express Company. In addition, the author acknowledges the support of the Business Roundtable. Needless to say, however, the author is solely responsible for the opinions he expresses in this paper, which do not always agree with those of the persons or organizations listed. The author also wishes to thank Ross Denton, graduate student in law at the University of Michigan, for his able assistance with the text and footnotes.

service providers located or controlled primarily outside the nation's borders.[5] The time seems propitious for the development of an international regime to try to inhibit the purely protectionist impulses of governments before they lead to national regulatory systems that become hardened and difficult to dismantle.

These considerations were among those that led the participants in the ministerial meeting of the General Agreement on Tariffs and Trade in September 1986 at Punta del Este, Uruguay, to include in the declaration launching the eighth major GATT round of trade negotiations provisions for negotiating agreements on trade in services. Those provisions were certainly not without controversy, and the compromise language adopted is not entirely clear on a number of significant matters. But it is clear that the Uruguay round negotiators are charged with the responsibility of addressing the problems of world trade in services, as a counterpart to the existing world framework for trade in products.[6]

World welfare might be considerably enhanced by a system that would forestall or dismantle some of the more purely protectionist governmental regulation of services. We cannot always assume, however, that the familiar and traditional economic doctrines relating to trade in goods, such as the doctrine of comparative advantage (itself under some attack), apply equally to trade in services, although certainly some respected economists seem to think that they do.[7]

Because of the great variety of services, often involving no tangible property, and the difficulty of deciding when service activity crosses a border, the national or international regulation of services is very difficult. It is also difficult to develop a new legal system for services. The GATT, for example, is often cited as a possible model for services trade.[8] Because of the great differences between trade in services and trade in goods, however, it is doubtful that the GATT model can be followed closely. The purpose of this paper is to explore a legal and institutional structure that might be used to develop an international discipline on services trade and to compare that structure with the GATT model.

Obviously any international discipline entails some yielding of sovereignty by national governments. The GATT already imposes some constraints on what sovereign governments are allowed to do. A GATT for services would likewise impose constraints. At almost every step of considering a structure for services, policy makers must confront the trade-off between, on the one hand, the broader goals of world and national economic welfare and, on the other hand, the legitimate desires of national leaders to retain as many governmental tools as possible to address the needs of their constituents. Sometimes these trade-offs will strengthen international discipline, yielding sovereignty. At other times, however, the forces making for the retention of power by national governments will be too great. In thinking about a structure for services, we must be sensitive to these trade-offs. International control is not always better than the less centralized decisions of governments that are closer to their constituents.[9]

In this paper I explore these basic institutional questions about potential international agreements for trade in services in the context of the Uruguay round of trade negotiations. I do not examine specific service sectors or possible detailed rules for specific service issues. Those issues are much more ably addressed by other writers and experts who are knowledgeable about various service sectors.[10]

The ideas and reflections expressed in this paper stem partly from considerable discussion about services trade with other scholars, government officials, and policy makers. I make no special claim to originality for many of these ideas, although some of my perspectives may differ from those of other experts and reflect basic policy questions that appear to be unresolved.[11] The ideas in this paper also stem from several decades of writing, thinking, and practicing in the area of international trade and the GATT. The history of the GATT is rich in analogies and potentially instructive experiences. But the GATT is a flawed instrument for many reasons, and one of the objectives of services negotiations should be to avoid its mistakes and flaws.[12]

Many points discussed here are put forward tentatively and with no claim to absolute truth. Many are matters of judgment, and their application will often depend on constraints of negotiating context and pressures, as well as on the gathering of much additional information not currently available to me or, in some cases, to policy makers. I hope that this discussion can serve as a checklist of issues and policy considerations that should at least be taken into account during the Uruguay round.

One policy direction implicit in the discussions throughout this paper should be made explicit. There are strong reasons why international institutions concerned with economic relations should primarily follow a rule-oriented rather than a power-oriented approach. In previous writings I have explained this as follows:

It seems to me that diplomatic techniques can be roughly categorized into two groups: (1) the technique we can call "power oriented"; and (2) the technique which we might call "rule oriented." Power oriented techniques suggest a diplomat asserting, subtly or otherwise, the power of the nation he represents. In general, such a diplomat prefers negotiation as a method of settling matters, because he can bring to bear the power of his nation to win advantage in particular negotiations, whether the power be manifested as promised aid, movement of an aircraft carrier, trade concessions, exchange rate changes, or the like. Needless to say, often large countries tend to favor this technique more than do small countries; the latter being more inclined to institutionalized ·or "rule oriented" structures of international activity. . . .

A rule oriented approach, by way of contrast, would suggest that a rule be formulated which makes broad policy sense for the benefit of the world and the parties concerned, and then there should be an attempt to develop institutions to insure the highest possible degree of adherence to that rule. . . .

All diplomacy, and indeed all government, involves a mixture of these techniques. To a large degree, the history of civilization may be described as a gradual evolution from a power oriented approach, in the state of nature, towards a rule oriented approach. However, never is the extreme in either case reached. In modern western democracies, as we know them, power continues to play a major role, particularly political power of voter acceptance, but also to a lesser degree economic power such as labor unions or large corporations. . . .

. . . a particularly strong argument exists for pursuing evenhandedly and with a fixed direction the progress of international economic affairs towards a rule oriented approach. Apart from the advantages which accrue generally to international affairs through a rule oriented approach—less reliance on raw power and the temptation to exercise it or flex one's muscles which can get out of hand; a fairer break for the smaller countries, or at least a perception of greater fairness; the development of agreed procedures to achieve the necessary compromises; in ECONOMIC affairs there are additional reasons. . . .

Economic affairs tend (at least in peace time) to affect more citizens directly than may be the case for political and military affairs. Particularly as the world becomes more economically interdependent, more and more private citizens find their jobs, their businesses, and their quality of life affected if not controlled by forces from outside their country's boundaries. Thus they are more affected by the economic policy pursued by their own country on their behalf. In addition, the relationships become increasingly complex—to the point of being incomprehensible to even the brilliant human mind.

As a result, citizens assert themselves, at least within a democracy, and require their representatives and government officials to respond to their needs and their perceived complaints. The result of this is increasing citizen participation, and more parliamentary or congressional participation in the processes of international economic policy, thus restricting the degree of power and discretion which the Executive possesses. This makes international negotiations and bargaining increasingly difficult.

However, if citizens are going to make their demands be heard and have their influence, a "power oriented" negotiating process (often requiring secrecy, and executive discretion so as to be able to formulate and implement the necessary compromises) becomes more difficult if not impossible. Consequently, the only appropriate way to turn seems to be toward a rule oriented system, whereby the various layers of citizens, parliaments, executives and international organizations will all have their inputs, arriving tortuously to a rule, which however, when established will enable business and other decentralized decision makers to rely upon the stability and predictability of governmental activity in relation to the rule.[13]

Trade in Goods: The GATT Structure Reviewed

Since the GATT is often cited as a model for international discipline in economic relations, a brief review of its nature and outlines is worthwhile. The most important fact about the GATT—or more broadly what we can term the "GATT system," so as to embrace the many separate treaty instruments and practices that together form its legal structure—is that it was never intended to be what it has become. The original idea, just after World War II, was to create an organizational counterpart to the World Bank and the International Monetary Fund (IMF), to be called the International Trade Organization (ITO). The GATT was to be merely an agreement on tariffs, appended to and administered by the ITO. In theory the GATT was not an organization. It therefore does not have "members"; accepting governments are "contracting parties."[14]

In due course, however, the ITO idea failed. The final draft ITO charter completed at Havana in 1948 was not accepted by the U.S. Congress, and no other country was willing to bind itself to that charter without its application to the preeminent economic power, the United States. The GATT, however, was accepted by the United States (through the Protocol of Provisional Application) under authority

7

granted to the U.S. president in the 1945 extension of the Reciprocal Trade Agreements Act. Congress did not need to approve the GATT.[15]

The GATT was thus thrust into the position of the principal international institution for controlling trade, even though it had inadequate institutional provisions (such as for rule making, voting, dispute settlement, new members, a secretariat). These constitutional infirmities are the source even today of significant problems of the GATT system. Some of them have been extensively commented on and are part of the agenda for the new GATT round of trade negotiations.[16]

Substantively the core of GATT can be described as including obligations that relate to trade in goods (but only in goods) and that constrain government regulatory actions. Only a very few GATT obligations could be said to apply even by implication to business firms or individuals.[17] The GATT was designed to limit what governments could do to create hurdles to trade across borders. The obligations include the following:

• negotiated tariff "binding," item by item, contained in a schedule for each GATT contracting party, with each party obligated to avoid applying a tariff in excess of the "bound rate" contained in its schedule[18]
• a most-favored-nation (MFN) obligation, requiring each GATT contracting party to treat goods originating in any other contracting party on a basis equal to (or "at least as favorable" as) the treatment afforded to the most favored GATT contracting party[19]
• a national treatment obligation, requiring each GATT contracting party to treat imported goods, once they have crossed the border (cleared the border "customs" process), no less favorably than it treats goods produced domestically[20]
• a broad prohibition on the use of quotas with a few exceptions (for example, for balance-of-payments reasons)[21]
• a series of "due process" obligations constraining the manner in which governments apply their tariffs and customs regulations, requiring due notice, realistic (not arbitrary) valuation methods, opportunity to appeal, and so on[22]
• obligations permitting but channeling the use of antidumping and countervailing duties (to offset dumping margins and subsidies)[23]
• obligations constraining the kinds of subsidies that can be used to benefit goods that are exported or compete with imports[24]

The GATT agreement also contains a series of exceptions, some of which arguably make serious inroads in the obligations listed. Most prominent among the exceptions are those for national security, health and welfare and intellectual property measures, customs unions and free trade areas, certain agricultural programs, certain measures taken by developing countries to aid economic development, and escape clause measures to slow imports and allow domestic industries to adjust to competition.[25]

In addition, because the GATT agreement has never come into force, instead being applied through the Protocol of Provisional Application, grandfather rights exempt some countries from parts of the GATT obligations that conflict with "existing legislation."[26] For certain historical reasons the GATT provides in Article XXXV a clause allowing any country to "opt out" of a GATT relationship with any other GATT country, a privilege exercisable in theory at one time only—when one or the other country enters the GATT.[27] These two exceptions in particular have caused troublesome problems for the GATT and its ability to discipline international economic relations effectively. When these are added to the longer list of other exceptions, the pattern of escapes provides sufficient opportunity for governments to evade their GATT responsibilities to evoke the criticism that GATT is meaningless (which it is not).

Furthermore, partly because of the weakness of the GATT institutional provisions, particularly the procedures for settling disputes and for keeping rules up to date with rapidly changing international patterns of economic activities (such as evolving ideas of "industrial policy"), even those rules that technically apply are sometimes avoided.[28]

Despite all this, the GATT has been remarkably successful in holding its own as an effective international system to keep pressure on governments to avoid at least the most damaging protectionist measures. Certainly it has been far more successful than could have been predicted in the early period after the failure of the ITO. A key question, however, is how much longer the GATT system can cope with a world that is economically very different from that for which it was designed. The GATT membership, for example, has increased more than fourfold and now includes countries with a much greater variety of economic systems and stages of development.[29] The GATT was essentially designed for market economies and has great difficulty coping successfully with state-trading, nonmarket economies and even some activities of modern market economy governments, such as industrial policies based on targeting strategies. Even modest differences in economic structure, such as customary differences in the debt-equity structures of firms, can have significant effects on

9

trade flows and entrepreneurial behavior, some of which is perceived as unfair by domestic industries competing with goods from other systems.[30]

Policy Goals for a Services Agreement

The complexity, defects, and problems of the GATT system for trade in goods, when added to the much greater variety and complexity of trade in services, result in a web of crosscurrents that is so difficult to organize by international rules that any person, no matter how expert, must approach the subject with great caution. Indeed, in my view it will not be possible, within a few years or the time span of one GATT negotiating round, to build a complete structure of such rules. It seems better to recognize this and to focus on the institutional structure that could be established. Such a structure should allow the satisfactory evolution of substantive rules over a period of some decades, so that they would enhance the broader goals of increasing world welfare while retaining for sovereign governments enough power and decision-making authority to administer to their constituents' reasonable needs.

It appears dangerous and probably impractical, for example, to try to design sweeping rules, such as a broad national treatment obligation, that apply to all services, regardless of sector. The details of how best to design an international discipline for the banking sector, for example, may differ substantially from that endeavor for the insurance or engineering services sector.[31] Different sectors have different rates of technological advance and degrees of importance to national security or other sovereign goals and rely on substantially different business structures (compare banks with airlines). In addition, the amount of national regulation already in place and thus the interest group support for the status quo vary greatly from sector to sector, as well as from country to country.

What is very important, however, is to think carefully about the basic constitutional structure of a system that can contribute to the beneficial evolution of more detailed rules. Such a structure should be relatively nonthreatening so as to encourage broad participation. It should provide a framework for gathering information and carrying out detailed analyses and studies to facilitate future rule making. It should establish a legal structure to reinforce the evolution and predictability of rules relating to service trade in a variety of sectors. While encouraging broad participation so that holdouts do not jeopardize the willingness of participants to enter into meaningful commitments, it should allow subgroups of like-minded nations to forge ahead with sets of obligations that not all members are yet prepared to accept. In other words, it should as far as feasible avoid the most-favored-nation foot-dragger problem experienced in the GATT and in other contexts.[32]

This is an ambitious agenda. Clearly some of these goals will not be fully or satisfactorily achieved, at least in the short run. Focusing on long-term constitutional issues does not always encourage firms or groups interested in short-term bottom-line results. There is therefore always a risk of losing support for the services negotiations from some constituent groups. Thus compromises between the longer-term goals and shorter-term results are probably inevitable. What must be preserved, however, is the goal of achieving, preferably by the end of the Uruguay round, a legal-institutional structure that provides both some useful rules for specific service sector trade and a framework for further decades of developing rules and discipline for service trade.

In carrying out these policy objectives, past experience, especially that of the GATT, will be extremely useful. Thus I frequently refer to that experience. It seems particularly desirable to avoid the institutional defects as well as the problems posed by the "grandfather" exceptions that have troubled the GATT. Likewise, there are good arguments for trying to achieve a broad and varied membership and to avoid the characterization of a "rich man's club" by drawing developing countries as deeply into the process as possible.

Notes

1. The General Agreement on Tariffs and Trade (GATT) is the principal treaty dealing with international trade in goods. An extensive literature on the GATT includes a number of works by this author: *World Trade and the Law of GATT* (Indianapolis, Ind.: Bobbs-Merrill, 1969); *Legal Problems of International Economic Relations: Cases, Materials, and Text on the National and International Regulation of International Economic Relations* (St. Paul, Minn.: West, 1977), 2d ed. with Professor William J. Davey (St. Paul, Minn.: West, 1986); and *Implementing the Tokyo Round: National Constitutions and International Economic Rules*, with Mitsuo Matsushita and Jean-Victor Louis (Ann Arbor: University of Michigan Press, 1984). Other works of interest include Edmond McGovern, *International Trade Regulation*, 2d ed. (Exeter: Globefield Press, 1986); Robert Hudec, *The GATT Legal System and World Trade Diplomacy* (New York: Praeger, 1975); and Kenneth Dam, *The GATT Law and International Economic Organization* (Chicago: University of Chicago Press, 1970).

2. A number of international organizations regulate or monitor service trade. Among the more important are the Organization for Economic Cooperation and Development (OECD), the United Nations Conference on Trade and Development (UNCTAD), and the International Chamber of Commerce. Numerous sector-specific organizations also regulate trade in services, such

as the International Civil Aviation Organization, the International Telecommunications Union, the International Maritime Organization, the International Labor Office, and the World Intellectual Property Organization.

3. In 1983 services constituted 71 percent of gross domestic product in the United States, 62 percent in France, 59 percent in the Federal Republic of Germany, 65 percent in Japan, and 57 percent in the United Kingdom. See Mario Kakabadse, *International Trade in Services: Prospects for Liberalization in the 1990's*, Atlantic Paper no. 64 (London: Croom Helm, 1987).

Statistics concerning trade in services are sparse and underdeveloped. See, for example, Robert Stern and Bernard Hoekman, "Issues and Data Needs for GATT Negotiations on Services," *World Economy*, vol. 10 (1987), pp. 39–60. The reliability of such statistics is also much debated. Many commentators think that figures, sparse as they are, tend to underestimate trade in services because of several factors: the "voluntary" reporting of statistics; the fact that many services are traded within a corporate entity or group of entities; and the fact that many traded services are reported as part of the products to which they relate.

4. There is some academic debate about what constitutes trade in services. See Gary Sampson and Richard Snape, "Identifying the Issues in Trade in Services," *World Economy*, vol. 8 (1985); Stern and Hoekman, "Issues and Data Needs"; William Diebold and Helena Stalson, "Negotiating Issues in International Services Transactions," in William Cline, ed., *Trade Policy in the 1980s* (Washington, D.C.: Institute for International Economics, 1983), pp. 582–86; Bernard Ascher and Obie Whichard, in Orio Giarini, ed., *The Emerging Service Economy* (Oxford: Pergamon Press, 1987). See also Deepak Nayyar, "International Trade in Services: Implications for Developing Countries" (Exim Bank Commencement Day Annual Lecture, 1986).

5. See actions brought under section 301 of the Trade Act of 1974 against Taiwan concerning restrictions of licenses for motion pictures (Docket no. 301–45, 49 FR 18056) and against South Korea concerning insurance services (Docket no. 301–51, 50 FR 37609). See also a similar case brought against South Korea in 1979 (Docket no. 301–20, 44 FR 75246) and the discussion in Bart Fisher and Ralph Steinhardt, "Section 301 of the Trade Act of 1974: Protection for U.S. Exporters of Goods, Services, and Capital," *Journal of Law and Policy in International Business*, vol. 14 (1982), pp. 469–690.

6. See Ministerial Declaration, GATT Press Release GATT/1396, September 25, 1986.

7. See Alan Deardorff, "Comparative Advantage and International Trade in Services," and Gene Grossman and C. Shapiro, "Normative Issues Raised by International Trade and Technology Services," both in Robert M. Stern, ed., *Trade and Investment Services: Canada/US Perspectives* (Toronto: University of Toronto Press, 1985). See also Giarini, *The Emerging Service Economy*, pt. 1, "The Economics of Services." See also H. Peter Gray, "A Negotiating Strategy for Trade in Services," *Journal of World Trade Law*, vol. 17 (1983), pp. 378–79; Brian Hindley and Alastair Smith, "Comparative Advantage and Trade in Services," *World Economy*, vol. 7 (1984), pp. 369–89; and B. Herman and B. van Holst, *International Trade in Services: Some Theoretical and Practical Problems* (Rotterdam: Netherlands Economic Institute, 1985).

8. See also Kakabadse, *International Trade in Services;* Richard Rivers, Valerie Slater, and Angela Paolini, "Putting Services on the Table: The New GATT Round," *Stanford Journal of International Law,* vol. 23 (1987), pp. 18–21: and Clark, "Services and the General Agreement on Tariffs and Trade" (Discussion Paper, International Economics Programme for Institute for Research on Public Policy, Ottawa, 1986).

9. The reader interested in this point can find some elaboration in Jackson, *Legal Problems,* pp. 1242–43.

10. The American Enterprise Institute has prepared a series of books (published by Ballinger in 1988) dealing with trade in particular services sectors. See Geza Feketekuty, *International Trade in Services: An Overview and Blueprint for Trade Negotiations."* Other contributions on specific areas include aviation, banking, insurance, professional services, shipping, and telecommunications. See also Giarini, *The Emerging Service Economy,* pt. 2.

11. See, for example, "National Treatment Obligation" below.

12. See works mentioned in note 1. See also John H. Jackson, "The Crumbling Institutions of the Liberal Trade Order," *Journal of World Trade Law,* vol. 12 (1978), p. 93; and John H. Jackson, "The Birth of the GATT-MTN System: A Constitutional Appraisal," *Journal of Law and Policy in International Business,* vol. 12 (1980), p. 21.

13. See Jackson, "Crumbling Institutions," pp. 98–101; and Jackson, *World Trade.*

14. See Jackson, *World Trade,* chap. 5.

15. See ibid.; and John H. Jackson, "The General Agreement on Tariffs and Trade in United States Domestic Law," *Michigan Law Review,* vol. 66 (1967), p. 249.

16. See Ministerial Declaration pt. I, E. The improvement of the dispute settlement system has been seen by the U.S. administration as a major and crucial objective of the new round. See, for example, (1985) 2 ITR 1555. See also testimony of Ambassador Clayton Yeutter before the Subcommittee on Trade, Committee on Ways and Means, U.S. House of Representatives, September 25, 1986.

17. See General Agreement on Tariffs and Trade, Article XVII. See also Jackson, *World Trade,* chap. 12.4, p. 289, and chap. 14.4, pp. 343–45.

18. See Jackson, *World Trade,* chap. 10; Jackson, *Legal Problems,* chap. 6.3; and Dam, *GATT Law,* pp. 17, 18, 25–55.

19. See Jackson, *World Trade,* chap. 11; and Jackson, *Legal Problems,* chap. 7.

20. See Jackson, *World Trade,* chap. 12; and Jackson, *Legal Problems,* chap. 8.

21. See Jackson, *World Trade,* chap. 13; and Jackson, *Legal Problems,* chap. 6.4.

22. See Jackson, *World Trade;* and Jackson, *Legal Problems,* chap. 6.

23. See Jackson, *World Trade,* chap. 16; and Jackson, *Legal Problems,* chap. 10.1, 10.2.

24. See Jackson, *World Trade,* chap. 15; and Jackson, *Legal Problems,* chap. 10.3.

25. See Jackson, *World Trade,* pt. 3.

26. See ibid., chap. 3, p. 60; and Jackson, *Legal Problems,* chap. 5.4(c).

27. See Jackson, *World Trade,* chap. 4.6, chap. 22, esp. 22.3, p. 549. See also

Jackson, *Legal Problems*, pp. 130–31, 927. In 1951 the contracting parties decided that the United States and Czechoslovakia should be free to suspend their obligations with respect to one another (BISD II/36 [1952]). The United States has also placed embargoes on Cuba under the Foreign Assistance Act of 1963 (22 USC 2370[a]) and Nicaragua under the International Emergency Economic Powers Act (50 USC 1701).

28. The prime example has been the use by the GATT and some countries of tariff surcharges for balance-of-payments reasons. In 1965 a paper written by the GATT secretariat argued for the use of tariff rather than quota restrictions during balance-of-payments crises (GATT Doc. Com. TD/F/W.3). See Jackson, *Legal Problems*, chap. 11.4(b). See also McGovern, "International Trade Regulation," 10.1.

29. In November 1987 the GATT had ninety-five contracting parties: twenty-one industrial countries, sixty-eight developing countries, and six nonmarket economies.

30. This point is developed more fully in Jackson, *Legal Problems*, pp. 648–52, 1241–46.

31. See note 10.

32. John H. Jackson, "Equality and Discrimination in International Economic Law (XI): The General Agreement on Tariffs and Trade," *British Yearbook of World Affairs* (1983), p. 224; and John H. Jackson, "Multilateral and Bilateral Negotiating Approaches for the Conduct of United States Trade Policies," in Robert M. Stern, ed., *U.S. Trade Policies in a Changing World Economy* (Cambridge, Mass.: MIT Press, 1987). See also Jan Tumlir, *Protectionism: Trade Policy in Democratic Societies* (Washington, D.C.: American Enterprise Institute, 1985), chap. 2.

2
Structure of a Constitution for Services Trade

Relation to the GATT

Services trade should not and cannot realistically be incorporated into the GATT agreement. The notion of amending the GATT briefly so that it would apply not only to products but also to services would not be wise for a number of reasons.

First, amending the GATT is very difficult, requiring two-thirds (and for some purposes unanimous) consent of the existing contracting parties (currently ninety-five). Thus countries that oppose an international services discipline would be in a position to exact concessions and compromises that might considerably water down the endeavor. This reasoning is why, in the Tokyo round, nations opted to rely primarily on side codes or separate agreements rather than amend the GATT.[1]

Second, the GATT has inadequate institutional provisions. These would simply carry over to services issues some of the most serious problems of the GATT. This would be particularly true of core questions such as dispute settlement procedures, voting, new members and their status, and methods of developing new rules and keeping them up to date.[2]

Third, it would be very threatening and probably politically unacceptable to apply many of the GATT obligations in an indefinite and ambiguous way to all service sectors, known and unknown. Nations would find a compelling political need to examine in detail how particular GATT obligations, such as national treatment or rules on subsidies, would apply to each sector of services (banking, insurance, engineering, law, medicine, the economics profession, education, films, television, theater, consulting for government agencies, advertising, investment and securities, and so on). In many of these sectors information is not readily available. No nation is likely to be willing to accept broad blank-check obligations applying to future unknown

15

activities as well as to little understood current activities. In addition, it is not entirely clear that world welfare would be enhanced by typical GATT rules of liberal trade in all service sectors. Intellectual property issues, for example, may require restricting trade to enhance longer-run world welfare.[3]

Fourth, it would be advantageous to experiment with rules for a few service sectors before imposing similar rules on other, lesser-known sectors.

The most difficult and threatening GATT obligation is, of course, that of national treatment, which requires nations to treat imports as favorably as domestic products. When applied to services, it would require nations to apply their regulations in a manner not less favorable to service providers from other nations than to domestic providers. Many nations would hesitate to agree to a strong national treatment obligation in many service sectors, at least without some experience of how that obligation might affect its tools for governing. Countries with nationalized banks, for example, would have problems with an obligation that foreign banks be treated no less favorably than domestic banks. In a number of other sectors, such as telecommunications, secrecy issues would come into play to reinforce national fears of international rules. Moreover, for some services effective access to a foreign market requires a "right of establishment" that raises issues of longstanding controversy.[4]

The GATT subsidy rules could also be very troublesome. Subsidies, though often misused, are a central tool of governments. Subsidy issues perplex the policy makers and negotiators in connection with trade in products.[5] That perplexity would be compounded in relation to service sectors, many of which are less well understood, and would involve intangibles that are more difficult to administer or to evaluate.[6]

In addition, traditional rules for products do not fit some kinds of services. Some services can easily be provided by establishments located outside the consuming nation. For other services some sort of establishment in the consuming nation is necessary for effective delivery, and this raises a host of traditional and nontraditional international law questions, such as the right of establishment, protection of foreign investment, and employment rules.[7] Many concerns of developing countries in recent decades about the activities of multinational corporations will manifest themselves in opposition to rules such as national treatment. Even developed nations worry about the relative ease with which multinational corporations seem able to evade government regulation.[8]

The Structure of a Constitution

The various considerations mentioned have led a number of persons to suggest a services constitution with at least two layers of agreement. The objective would be to establish a legal and institutional structure for international trade in services that would make it easy and nonthreatening for countries to participate at least in the first or top layer of obligations. The top layer would contain institutional measures (including the supervisory body, a secretariat, decision-making rules, and dispute settlement procedures) along with some relatively modest obligations. Some substantive provisions in this layer might be phrased as "principles," "objectives," or "goals." The basic purpose of the layer would be to establish a legal-institutional structure that would facilitate the evolution of specific sector agreements with detailed rules.

Many have termed this top layer the umbrella agreement. It would be complemented by specific service sector agreements (SSAs) or codes, such as a code for banking and one for insurance. The umbrella agreement might also contain an intermediate layer of more significant concrete obligations concerning a list of service sectors. This layer might be constructed as an optional title, or optional protocol (as in a number of international agreements, especially in the human rights area). The optional title, which we might call the general services protocol, might also be legally designed as simply another SSA but one that applied to a number of sectors in the absence of a specific SSA. The general services protocol might contain a few key obligations such as a most-favored-nation obligation and some form of national treatment but might apply only to specified service sectors (to avoid the blank-check problem). It might also be worded so that whenever a more detailed SSA was ultimately adopted for a specific sector, that SSA would prevail over the general services protocol.

The final layer of obligations would be contained in a series of SSAs. Each agreement would be devoted to one sector and tailored to the particular needs and complexities of that sector. It would be understood that not all members of the umbrella agreement would need to join any particular sector agreement, but normally sector agreement membership would have some advantages that would not accrue automatically to countries that did not accept the agreement.

At the outset it might be feasible to negotiate only four or five sector agreements. Time and negotiating resources, as well as political acceptability, would constrain the number of sectors that could be covered. The umbrella code might include a framework for negotiating sector codes as well as rules about how the sector agreements relate to the umbrella agreement. So that an umbrella agreement would not be too hollow, some countries—such as those of the Organization for Economic Cooperation and Development—might decide among themselves, as a negotiating strategy, that the umbrella agreement would not come into force unless a specified number of sector agreements came into force. That might depend on a minimum number of acceptances of the sector agreements.

Relation to U.S. Law and Other National Laws

The international structure for an institution and obligations concerning trade in services should be considered in relation to the law of the United States and other key countries, such as those of the European Economic Community (EEC). The U.S. law in relation to the GATT has always been troubled; occasionally incorrect statements have been made that the GATT is not a binding legal instrument or that it has never been correctly approved under U.S. constitutional law.[9] This can be contrasted with the situation for the World Bank and the International Monetary Fund, which are covered under the U.S. Bretton Woods Agreement Act of 1945.[10]

In that act Congress authorized U.S. participation in the IMF and the World Bank and laid down rules governing U.S. representation in those organizations and specifying that some subjects (such as amendment or changing the par value of the dollar) would require the permission of Congress. Even if a set of services agreements were to be approved in the United States through fast-track legislative procedures, Congress would probably want some constraints on the executive and its relation to the new institution analogous to those in the Bretton Woods Agreement Act.[11] Some thought should be given to the appropriate framing of such constraints. It might be appropriate to prescribe the method by which Congress would approve future sector agreements negotiated under the umbrella agreement, and Congress might be willing to apply a fast-track procedure to such approvals.

Notes

1. See John H. Jackson with Mitsuo Matsushita and Jean-Victor Louis, *Implementing the Tokyo Round: National Constitutions and International Economic Rules* (Ann Arbor: University of Michigan Press, 1984), chap. 4.

2. John H. Jackson, "The Birth of the GATT-MTN System: A Constitutional Appraisal," *Journal of Law and Policy in International Business*, vol. 12

(1980), p. 21; and John H. Jackson, "Anticipating Trade Policy in 1987," *Looking Ahead* (National Planning Association), vol. 9 (1987), pp. 1–7.

3. See Gene Grossman and C. Shapiro, "Normative Issues Raised by International Trade and Technology Services," in Robert M. Stern, ed., *Trade and Investment Services: Canada/US Perspectives* (Toronto: University of Toronto Press, 1985).

4. See Mario Kakabadse, *International Trade in Services: Prospects for Liberalization in the 1990's*, Atlantic Paper no. 64 (London: Croom Helm, 1987), sec. 3; and Jonathan David Aronson and Peter F. Cowhey, *Trade in Services: A Case for Open Markets* (Washington, D.C.: American Enterprise Institute, 1984), pp. 25–26.

5. Gary Hufbauer and Joanna Shelton Erb, *Subsidies in International Trade* (Washington, D.C.: Institute of International Economics/MIT, 1984); Gary Hufbauer, "Subsidy Issues after the Tokyo Round," in William Cline, ed., *Trade Policy in the 1980s* (Washington, D.C.: Institute for International Economics, 1983); Daniel Tarullo, "The MTN Subsidies Code: Agreement without Consensus," in Seymour Rubin and Gary Hufbauer, eds., *Emerging Standards of International Trade and Investment* (Totowa, N.J.: Rowman and Allanheld, 1984). See also U.S. Congress, Joint Economic Committee, Subcommittee on Trade, Productivity, and Economic Growth, *Hearings: How to Save the International Trading System*, pt. 1, April 26, 1984; pt. 2, June 12, 1984; pt. 3, September 20, 1984; see esp. pt. 1, pp. 3–50.

6. See notes 3 and 4 to chapter 1.

7. See the AEI series, note 10 to chapter 1.

8. The extraterritorial application of regulatory laws is an immensely complex and pervasive topic. See Griffin, "A Primer on Extraterritoriality," *International Business Lawyer* (1985), p. 23, and *Journal of Law and Policy in International Business*, vol. 15 (1983), p. 1095. See also US v. Aluminium Co. of America (148 F.2d 416); Timberlane Lumber Co. v. Bank of America (549 F.2d 597); and the Laker litigation as described in *Journal of Law and Policy in International Business*, vol. 17 (1985), p. 157.

9. See John H. Jackson, *World Trade and the Law of GATT* (Indianapolis, Ind.: Bobbs-Merrill, 1969), chap. 3.2; and John H. Jackson, *Legal Problems of International Relations* (St. Paul, Minn.: West, 1977), chap. 5.4(c).

10. See Bretton Woods Agreement Act, as amended (22 UCSA 286–86x).

11. See Jackson, *Legal Problems*, chap. 5.4; and Jackson, *Implementing the Tokyo Round*, chap. 4, pp. 162–68. See also Harold Koh, "Congressional Control on Presidential Trademaking Policy after *INS v. CHADHA*," *New York University Journal of International Law and Politics*, vol. 18 (1986), pp. 1191–1233.

3
Possible Contents of
an Umbrella Agreement

The principal objective of an umbrella, or first-layer, agreement for services trade should be the broadest possible participation consistent with a structure that would promote beneficial evolution of rules for services trade. The subjects discussed in this chapter should be among those considered for inclusion in the first layer. In chapter 4 I turn briefly to a possible general services protocol, or second layer of obligations, which might well be included in the umbrella agreement but acceptance of which would be optional. Such a second layer should be constructed so as to offer some benefits to those who do accept. One possibility is to reserve most-favored-nation treatment for adherents to the optional protocol. A number of the other obligations could well fall back into the optional protocol if including them in the universal umbrella would cause too many nations to refrain from joining.

Statement of Objectives

Carefully phrased objectives can have a considerable effect on later interpretation and implementation of an agreement and in resolving disputes about it.[1] GATT objectives, which might be modified for services, are worded as follows:

> Recognizing that their relations in the field of trade and economic endeavour should be conducted with a view to raising standards of living, ensuring full employment and a large and steadily growing volume of real income and effective demand, developing the full use of the resources of the world and expanding the production and exchange of goods.
>
> Being desirous of contributing to these objectives by entering into reciprocal and mutually advantageous arrangements directed to the substantial reduction of tariffs and other barriers to trade and to the elimination of discriminatory treatment in international commerce.

A general objective of minimizing world tensions stemming from economic relations might be added. Other stated objectives might relate to the need to recognize the advantages of rules and predictability; the need for further study and gathering of information; the need to develop a framework for pragmatic evolution of rules for a wide variety of service sectors; the need to assist economic development in countries with lower standards of living; and the need to balance the advantages of national sovereignty against the advantages of international cooperation and discipline.

Institutional Measures

Supervisory Body. Provisions must be included for a highest supervisory body, called an assembly or contracting parties or the like. These provisions should address such questions as the seat of headquarters, the frequency of meetings, powers and competence, and especially voting.[2] Clearly consideration of these provisions must include their relation to the GATT. Presumably it would not be advisable simply to allow the existing GATT contracting parties to be the supervising body for the new services agreement, but the relationship between the GATT and a new services supervising group would need to be worked out. Does this imply an even broader group for both endeavors, such as a modified institutional structure along the lines of the ill-fated Organization for Trade Cooperation (OTC) of the mid-1950s? Or can the GATT and a new set of contracting parties for services share premises, staff, a secretariat, and other institutions?

The voting question will be particularly sensitive.[3] For decisions to be effective, they must be accepted by a reasonably large part of the real power that exists among members. At least for certain decisions a one-nation, one-vote procedure is not conducive to such effectiveness, since the powerful nations might sometimes be outvoted and then refuse to carry out the decisions effectively. The system does not need to cater exclusively to power, however, but should impose a sense of fairness and justice even on powerful nations.

Various combinations of voting structure should be examined. Obviously the weighted voting structure of the IMF or the World Bank is a model that must be considered. Voting might be weighted by participant countries' shares of the total international services trade. Combinations of weighted and one-nation, one-vote systems might be used to protect the less powerful from the more powerful. A council or other sub-body with representative membership can sometimes substitute for weighted voting. In a 100-nation organization, for example, a 20-nation council, with the five largest trading nations and representatives of several geographic regions and types of economic systems as members, might be joined with a two-thirds or three-fourths council voting requirement as a condition for adoption of certain kinds of decisions. The voting question relates intimately to the kinds of decisions to be made. A qualified voting pattern might be required for new rules, for budgets, and for certain waivers.

Voting on certain questions should probably be allowed only to subsets of the umbrella members. For example, powerful arguments and precedents support a rule that, in issues of legal interpretation or application of a subordinate sector agreement (not the umbrella agreement), only nations that have accepted the sector agreement should vote.[4] Yet allowing all umbrella nations to participate in debate on the subject might be valuable, so that nonsector parties would have their "day in court" concerning byproduct effects of specific sector rules and actions. Thus it might be efficient and beneficial to allow the umbrella supervisory body to supervise the sector agreements, rather than have a separate "committee of signatories" for each, as in the GATT, provided that voting on a measure be limited to nations that have accepted the sector agreement.

Smaller Steering and Policy Body. Since the umbrella supervisory body is not likely to meet frequently, a smaller body (such as the GATT council or the executive board of the IMF) will be necessary. Again voting and power distribution need to be considered.

Secretariat. Provision must be made for a secretariat and for a chief officer of the secretariat. Funding and budget obligations and decisions must be determined. One important question is whether to use the GATT secretariat or, more appropriately, to use a combined secretariat for both the GATT and the services agreement. Obviously many arguments favor that approach.

Membership. The processes of accepting new members and expelling members must be set forth. Should membership require a two-thirds vote or be open to all? Should expulsion follow gross defiance of obligations, as ruled by a dispute settlement panel and approved by two-thirds of the supervisory body?

Final Clauses. The traditional final clauses of a treaty must be framed: when it is to open for signature, its ratification, when it is to come into force (for example, when twenty countries, accounting for at least 25 percent of the international services trade total of all preparatory countries, have ratified it).

Dispute Settlement

It would be wise to provide carefully thought out procedures and institutions for resolution of all disputes about services trade, including issues arising under sector agreements or other related or subordinate treaties. The multiple procedures of the GATT are not beneficial since they allow "forum shopping," add to uncertainty, impose greater needs of expertise and staffing, are harder for the world's public to understand, and are more easily abused and manipulated.[5] A single procedure offers the best chance for a dispute settlement process to gain prestige, which is the real basis in international relations for potential effectiveness.

Such a procedure should have as its central feature a panel that would be charged with making impartial, third-party, well-reasoned, and published findings or determinations of whether certain actions by a nation are inconsistent with treaty obligations. The procedure should provide for secretariat services and a roster of potential panelists and should embrace the following obligations and steps:

- A general obligation should be imposed to consult with any other members of the services umbrella agreement on any matter related to trade in services, regardless of whether the matter is covered by a sector agreement or any other service rules under the system. The obligation should include the duty to provide reasonable information about actions or processes concerning services trade in any member nation. This step can be confidential and bilateral.

- An obligation should be imposed to cooperate in a process of mediation or conciliation supervised by a secretariat service if the consultation step does not result in a settlement of differences. The secretariat would assist the parties in achieving a resolution of their differences, a process that in the GATT is often unfortunately confused with other parts of the dispute settlement procedure.

- A panel procedure is needed, invocable as of right by any member of the services umbrella agreement, that will focus on coming to findings about the consistency of practices with legal treaty obligations, including those in specific sector agreements. (The unfortunately ambiguous language of GATT dispute settlement procedures, the "nullification or impairment" phrase, should be avoided.) The first two steps should be a prerequisite for this step. Measures for selecting panel members must guard against delaying tactics and ensure the panel's impartiality as well as its expertise. More detail than exists in the GATT is needed for procedures for fact and information gathering, for representation of interested parties other than the original disputants, for time limits, and for avoiding delay in publishing the panel's report. The panel need not be given power to recommend and should avoid conciliation efforts, which sometimes confuse panelists about their role of coming to an objective finding. Provision might be made for disputants to opt in favor of being bound by the panel report or giving the panel power to make recommendations or rule *ex aequo et bono* (on equitable rather than legal grounds), as is done for the world court. Without such an agreement, however, the panel's competence should exclude these results or activities.

• A political body of the organization, such as a council, the umbrella supervisory body, or a similar sector body, should have the power to approve or disapprove a report or send it back to be rewritten or to invoke a new panel process to reconsider a case. This process would provide a political or policy filter for the otherwise more strictly legal results of a panel. The panelists could then focus impartially on the legal questions. The political filter could invoke broader policy considerations, but only after the world knew the results of able thinking about the legal issues, so that those results became part of the broader considerations. This political filter might make it more palatable for nations to commit themselves to a meaningful dispute settlement process. Yet as time and experience operate to increase the prestige of the panel process, a panel report is more likely to have great weight in the political considerations.

• The final step would be consideration of potential sanctions or responding actions either by a complaining country or, in severe cases, by all members of the organization. It must not be assumed, however, that sanctions or retaliatory responses are essential for a dispute settlement process to be successful. In fact, the prime reason for the effectiveness of such a process is the willingness of nations, especially powerful nations, to implement the results of a panel report "voluntarily." They are more likely to do so if the process gains prestige and respect through experience and carefully framed impartial and reasoned reports. Sanctions are often not important. Nations realize that to ignore or flout a dispute settlement result will make it harder for them to use that procedure when they need it and will generally reduce the utility of treaty commitments.

Transparency Obligations

A prime candidate for the umbrella agreement is an obligation to report many kinds of information about governmental practices relating to services trade. This would help nations and the secretariat to study the problems of services trade, perhaps in preparation for developing new sector agreements or updating existing agreements. The consultation obligation is related to this one, but in that context information could remain confidential. A general obligation that would give the supervisory body the authority to require information on any matter relating to services trade within reasonable resources (probably with exceptions for national security, intellectual property, and proprietary business) would be extremely useful as part of the umbrella agreement. The supervisory body might be empowered to establish a transparency committee or other sub-body to act on its behalf and supervise the gathering and examination of data. It might also rule on disputes about what is required from member nations by the transparency obligations.

Regulatory Due Process

Closely related to transparency, but going beyond it, is the concept of regulatory due process. GATT Articles VII through IX contain some analogous measures for customs procedures.[6] It would be useful to have a general obligation in the umbrella agreement, applicable to all services trade, that all members must afford a certain fair standard of procedure in government dealing with foreign service providers. This obligation could include measures requiring fair notice, available information about regulations and procedures, the right of appeal to an impartial tribunal, and similar matters. These could be linked to the consultation and dispute settlement procedures of the umbrella agreement. Then national governments could raise matters on behalf of their service providers who felt aggrieved by the actions of another nation.

Relation to Sector Agreements

The umbrella agreement should include provisions that contemplate specific service sector agreements and spell out the relation of those agreements to the umbrella agreement.

Some provision should be made for the procedures by which sector agreements are to be negotiated. It might be made explicit that if sector negotiations fulfilled specified criteria, the umbrella secretariat would assist in negotiation and implementation. (A list of possible subjects to be considered for any sector agreement is discussed in chapter 4. The umbrella agreement might contain a similar checklist for negotiators.)

Certain criteria should be established in the umbrella agreement as prerequisites for a service sector agreement to be an "agreement under the services umbrella":

• Participation in negotiating the sector agreement should be open to all members of the umbrella. Any member must have an opportunity to be heard in any negotiation, so as to point out potential problems in an agreement that would affect its interests, even if it knows it would not accept the obligations of the new agreement.

• The subject matter must be services trade.

• The supervisory body or a sub-body such as a council must approve (or at least not disapprove) the negotiation, probably by some sort of specially qualified vote, which must give leeway to the desires of a relatively small group of like-minded nations to launch such a negotiation. (Otherwise nations will take their affairs elsewhere, outside the services umbrella.)

• The umbrella dispute settlement procedures must apply to the sector agreement rules and members.

• Sector agreement rules (even though later in time) should be subordinate to umbrella agreement rules, unless the umbrella agreement expressly allows sector agreements to deviate.[7]

• Membership in the sector agreement must be open to any member of the umbrella agreement, on the sole condition that the nation must accept the rules and discipline of the sector agreement to be a part of it.

As an agreement under the umbrella, the sector agreement would have various advantages:

• secretariat services of the umbrella
• dispute settlement procedures of the umbrella
• possible deviation from specified umbrella obligations that are made subject to approved sector agreements
• the transparency provided in the umbrella agreement
• an opportunity to deviate from an umbrella agreement most-favored-nation requirement
• in the absence of contrary provisions in the sector agreement, adoption of some of the technical final clauses and institutional measures of the umbrella agreement such as provision for new members, amendment, ratification, funding of secretariat services and other measures, and rules on observers and state succession

Most-Favored-Nation Provisions

A vital question is to what extent an umbrella agreement should set forth a most-favored-nation (MFN) obligation. A number of aspects need to be considered. Some persuasive arguments suggest that it may not be in the best interests of some major industrial countries to enter into MFN obligations, especially if those countries are already significantly more receptive to foreign business than most other umbrella agreement countries would be. A possibly attractive alternative, therefore, would be to omit the MFN obligation from the mandatory umbrella agreement but include it as part of the optional protocol on the basis that only those nations accepting the protocol would be entitled to receive MFN treatment. One problem is that a number of existing treaties (such as friendship, commerce, and navigation treaties) contain MFN obligations that apply in various forms to services trade or aspects of services trade, such as a right of establishment. Clarification of these legal interrelationships would be needed.

The MFN commitment has many merits: reducing distortions in trade and thus maximizing welfare, reducing rancor and tension among nations, and sometimes accelerating liberalization by generalizing to all members any particular liberalizing activities.[8] But an MFN obligation also creates the foot-dragger and free-rider problems. Attempts by small groups of nations to develop more advanced beneficial rules can be thwarted if those nations know they must offer the benefits of better rules to all member nations, regardless of whether the beneficiaries will reciprocate or will undertake the discipline of the rules. Attempts to get every nation signed up make the process vulnerable to one or two holdouts, and going ahead without the holdouts gives them a free ride.

Thus it seems clear that any general MFN requirement, whether located in the optional protocol or in the umbrella agreement, should make an exception for sector agreements. Nations that accept the discipline of a sector agreement should also receive the benefits. Nations that refuse the discipline can be denied the benefits. This is a form of "code-conditional MFN," similar to some controverted views of several of the Tokyo round GATT codes.[9] The controversy of the GATT about this matter should be avoided, and the umbrella agreement should make it clear that code conditionality is a standard exception to the general umbrella or optional MFN requirement. Of course, sector agreements can and should have a specific MFN requirement for national government activities in the sector concerned.

It may be that other exceptions to a general MFN clause would also be wise. They can at least be considered. There will also probably be a political need for some grandfather exceptions, at least during a transitional period. It would be wise to provide explicitly for these but to set a strict time limit, with a sensible decision-making process for renewal. Reporting or registration should also be required for every exception, to reduce controversy over the existence and extent of the exception. In addition, treaty reservations should be prohibited.

These provisions and limits on exceptions may apply more broadly than just in the MFN context. They also relate to a general waiver authority.

National Treatment Obligation

An important policy decision is whether to try to include in an umbrella agreement a national treatment obligation. This obligation, which would require a nation to treat foreign service providers at least as favorably as it treats its domestic service providers, is probably the core of meaningful international discipline of national regulation of trade in services. For some kinds of trade it also raises questions of the right of establishment or other measures necessary for effective business operations by foreign service providers.[10]

I think that it is politically unlikely and probably unwise for nations to impose a national treatment obligation on services trade generally, including unnamed or unknown service sectors. National leaders would understandably hesitate to enter into such a blank-check obligation, which could cut deeply into existing and future government regulations and tread on sovereign toes in a very uncomfortable way. To include such a requirement in an umbrella agreement might greatly inhibit the broad participation that could build toward meaningful evolution of sound rules in many sectors. It seems wiser to leave the national treatment obligation to particular definition and implementation in an optional protocol and to each sector agreement. Each sector will have special problems and features that can be dealt with in negotiating its agreement. The information available for many sectors is probably not adequate for a good understanding of how an umbrella national treatment clause would affect national systems.

Two qualifications of these thoughts might be offered. First, an umbrella agreement might contain some statement of a national treatment objective or principle, perhaps requiring nations to pursue a goal of national treatment "to the fullest extent possible." This provision might be coupled with transparency requirements, such as to report any situation in which foreign service providers are not treated as well as domestic providers and to respond meaningfully to requests for information along the same lines. It might also state goals of providing meaningful market access when mere national treatment might not be enough to ensure such access. In addition, some consideration should be given to de facto discrimination—where measures appear on their face to be nondiscriminatory but in fact operate to the detriment of foreign providers.

Second, as outlined in chapter 4, a special subgroup of the umbrella membership may be prepared to go further in accepting a national treatment obligation in an optional protocol. If so, such a second-tier membership could be designed as part of the umbrella agreement or as a separate agreement analogous to a sector agreement. Such an agreement could be governed by the same disciplines under the umbrella agreement as a sector agreement, except that it might apply to a number of service sectors rather than just one. Indeed, a negotiated set of national schedules of sectors could be envisaged as part of such a national treatment service agreement. In any event, the preparatory negotiators for the umbrella agreement could make it a prerequisite of the implementation of an umbrella agreement that at least several sector agreements (with appropriate national treatment obligations) come into effect.

The apparently successful agreements on services in the United States–Canada Free Trade Area notifications might suggest that a multilateral services umbrella can be more ambitious.[11] We must remember, however, that the United States and Canada have cultures, economies, and legal structures that are much more similar than those of probably any other members of the GATT. The enormous diversity among GATT members makes it unwise to conclude that the United States–Canada relation will be an effective model in a context of much greater diversity.

General Exceptions

It would probably be wise to specify in the umbrella agreement general exceptions that would apply not only to obligations of the umbrella agreement but also to any sector agreement unless it included explicit measures negating the general exception. GATT Articles XX and XXI contain exceptions that should be considered, such as health and welfare measures, monopoly policies and laws, intellectual property measures, and national security.[12] All of these, particularly national security, are troublesome and can lead to considerable dispute. Nevertheless, they are necessary. Thus it is wise to think through language and procedures that give national sovereigns some leeway but impose some constraints, such as the modified, or soft, MFN and national treatment commitments of GATT Article XX. Reporting and transparency requirements should be linked to these and any other exceptions.

The GATT has several particularly troublesome exceptions that must be considered by analogy for a services agreement. One is for free trade areas and customs unions.[13] Another is the GATT Article XXXV opt-out provision, under which any GATT contracting party or newly entering party can announce that it will not have a GATT treaty relationship with any other GATT party.[14] Although this option is

exercisable at only one time—the time when one of the parties enters
GATT—countries have severed trading relations with other GATT
parties or imposed embargoes on them at various other times in their
GATT relations.[15] Although such measures have uncertain legal status, these severances of trading relations have nevertheless been
implemented and tolerated. Recognizing the realities of international
relations, we might find it best to provide explicitly for a "total opt-
out" for national sovereignty or security reasons, if certain due notice
and transparency provisions are fulfilled.

Another GATT exception is the escape clause of Article XIX. By
analogy again, some thought should be given to whether a general
escape clause should be included in a services umbrella agreement,
applying also to sector agreements unless the sector agreement negates it.[16] Other exceptions to consider include waiver authority and
measures for developing countries.

Waiver Provisions

Since the future is so hard to foresee, it is useful (as GATT experience
demonstrates) to include a provision allowing obligations to be
waived. In the GATT a two-thirds vote is required for a waiver, and
there have been some interpretive problems about other requirements
for waivers.[17] A waiver provision in a services umbrella agreement
might include the following features:

• It should apply to all umbrella and sector obligations, unless a
sector agreement explicitly negates a waiver possibility for a named
obligation.
• It should require a special qualified vote and, for waiving a sector
agreement obligation, a special vote of the nations that have accepted
that agreement.
• Waivers should always be limited in time. The umbrella might
specify that unless a shorter period is otherwise stated, a waiver
expires after five years. Waivers should, however, be renewable under
the same procedure as originally granted.
• Reporting, annual review, and transparency requirements
should be part of every waiver. The umbrella agreement should
contain details to apply to every waiver not otherwise making provision for such details.

Measures for Developing Countries

Both for general policy reasons and as a recognition of political constraints, special provisions for developing countries will undoubtedly

be necessary.[18] The umbrella agreement might contain at least some general "aspirational" provisions and perhaps some clauses similar to articles in the Tokyo round GATT codes that provide special assistance to developing countries. Details might better be placed in sector agreements. The question of graduation, or time limits on special favors for developing countries, must be faced.

Clearly, developing countries will desire some recognition of infant industry arguments applied to some service sectors, such as banking, insurance, or stock and securities brokerage. Some of these desires will merit special consideration. Whether a legal exception for them should be placed in the umbrella agreement, however, is less clear. Disciplined supervisory mechanisms, perhaps with a time limit, might be considered. Some statement of which countries would be recognized as developing countries for these purposes should be included, perhaps with a list of countries.[19]

Reciprocity

Some thought should be given to whether it makes sense to articulate in any formal manner a notion of reciprocity in the development of rules for services.[20] The umbrella agreement might include at least general considerations on this question, perhaps only as part of the statement of objectives or more significantly as a general clause expressing an obligation to be motivated or not by ideas of reciprocity.

Final Clauses

A series of typical treaty final clauses will be needed, to cover questions of signature, ratification, implementation, and the like. A prohibition of treaty reservations (similar to that in the Law of the Sea treaty draft) would probably be advisable.

Existing International Service Agreements

Consideration will be needed of the relationship to the umbrella agreement and certain sector agreements of existing international agreements covering services (such as the agreements for the Intergovernmental Maritime Organization, the International Telecommunications Union, and the International Civil Aviation Organization).[21] Although we should understand the formidable political, interest group, and bureaucratic opposition possible, it might be wise to bring an existing agreement or organization into some formal relationship to the umbrella agreement, comparable to that of a sector agreement.

Notes

1. See Article 31 of the Vienna Convention on the Law of Treaties.

2. Pieter van Dijk, ed., *Supervisory Mechanisms in International Economic Organizations* (Boston: Kluwer, 1984). See also Henry Schermers, *International Institutional Law* (Rockville, Md.: Sijthoff and Noordhoff, 1980).

3. See John H. Jackson, *Legal Problems of International Relations* (St. Paul, Minn.: West, 1977), chap. 5.3(2); Joseph Gold, *Voting and Decisions* (Washington, D.C.: IMF, 1972); and Schermers, *International Institutional Law*, pp. 681–83.

4. The 1979 GATT most-favored-nation codes also limit the right of participation in the working of each code to the signatories of that code.

5. John H. Jackson, "The Birth of the GATT-MTN System: A Constitutional Appraisal," *Journal of Law and Policy in International Business*, vol. 12 (1980), p. 21.

6. See John H. Jackson, *World Trade and the Law of GATT* (Indianapolis, Ind.: Bobbs-Merrill, 1969), chap. 17; and Jackson, *Legal Problems*, chap. 6.2.

7. Normally, international law of treaties would provide that between parties to both treaties, the later in time would prevail in the event of conflict. See Article 59 of the Vienna Convention on Law of Treaties.

8. See note 32 to chapter 1.

9. See John H. Jackson with Mitsuo Matsushita and Jean-Victor Louis, *Implementing the Tokyo Round: National Constitutions and International Economic Rules* (Ann Arbor: University of Michigan Press, 1984), chap. 4, pp. 160–61; and Jackson, *Legal Problems*. The GATT itself has taken up a position on the matter. See 1979 declaration on the relationship between the MTN codes and the GATT, (1980) 26 BISD 201. See also the Indian complaint concerning zip fasteners, (1982) 28 BISD 113.

10. See Mario Kakabadse, *International Trade in Services: Prospects for Liberalization in the 1990's*, Atlantic Paper no. 64 (London: Croom Helm, 1987), p. 71.

11. See the Free Trade Agreement between the United States and Canada initialed October 4, 1987 (4 ITR 1210).

12. GATT Article XX provides so-called general exceptions, subject to soft most-favored-nation and national treatment obligations. The exceptions include measures for health, public morals, intellectual property protection, historic objects, monopoly policy, commodity agreements, and the like. Article XXI is an exception for certain measures necessary for national security.

13. See, for example, Jackson, *World Trade*, chap. 24; and Jackson, *Legal Problems*, chap. 7.3. See also Uster, "The MFN Customs Union Exception," *Journal of World Trade Law*, vol. 15 (1981), p. 377; and Kenneth Dam, "Regional Economic Arrangements and the GATT: The Legacy of a Misconception," *University of Chicago Law Review*, vol. 30 (1963), p. 615.

14. See note 27 to chapter 1.

15. Ibid. See particularly Jackson, *World Trade*, chap. 22.3, p. 549.

16. Regarding "safeguards" and the escape clause, see, for example, Jackson, *World Trade*, chap. 23; and Jackson, *Legal Problems*, chap. 9. See also Marco C. E. J. Bronckers, *Selective Safeguard Measures in Multilateral Trade Relations* (Boston: Kluwer, 1985); and Mark Koulen, "The Non-Discriminatory Interpretation of Article XIX(1): A Reply," *Legal Issues of European Integration*, vol. 9 (1983), p. 87.

17. See Jackson, *Legal Problems*, chap. 5.4(g). See also GATT Doc. L/403, September 7, 1955.

18. A group of less-developed countries (LDCs), including Brazil and India, were vehemently opposed to including services in the Uruguay round, preferring to keep service trade out of the liberal trade rules (see 2 ITR 1491 and 1516). See also testimony of Ambassador Clayton Yeutter before U.S. Congress, House Committee on Ways and Means, Subcommittee on Trade, September 25, 1986, esp. pp. 6–7, 13. Part IV of the GATT, as well as Article XVIII, makes special provision for developing countries. Both the 1973 ministerial declaration launching the Tokyo round of negotiations and the 1986 Punta del Este declaration launching the new multilateral trade negotiations refer to the necessity for special measures for developing countries. See Deepak Nayyar, "International Trade in Services: Implications for Developing Countries" (Exim Bank Commencement Day Annual Lecture, 1986). See also Jagdish Bhagwati, "Splintering and Disembodiment of Services and Developing Nations," *World Economy*, vol. 7 (1984), pp. 133–44; A. F. Ewing, "Why Freer Trade in Services Is in the Interest of Developing Countries," *Journal of World Trade Law*, vol. 19 (1985), pp. 147–69; and Koekkoek and De Leeuw, "The Application of GATT to International Trade in Services: General Considerations and LDCs," *Aussenwirtschaft*, vol. 42 (1987), pp. 65–84.

19. International Monetary Fund, *1987 Annual Report*, p. 174, lists forty-three countries, all members of the IMF and the World Bank, that are considered low-income countries, with annual per capita GDP of not more than $410. China and India are included. Other similar lists include that found in the UNCTAD *Handbook of International Trade and Development Statistics*, which in 1985 specified thirty-six less-developed countries (LDCs). Beneficiaries of the U.S. General System of Preferences (Title V of the Trade Act of 1974 as amended, see 19 USC 2461–2465 and 19 CFR 10.171 et seq.) are listed in the annex to 19 USC 2462 setting out Executive Order 11888 as amended. The criteria necessary for listing as a recipient under the GSP scheme are found in 19 USC 2462(c).

20. See William Cline, "'Reciprocity': A New Approach to World Trade Policy?" *Policy Analyses in International Economics* (Institute for International Economics), vol. 2 (1982); Edmund Dell, "Of Free Trade and Reciprocity," *World Economy*, vol. 9 (1986), p. 125; and reply by Brian Hindley and Alasdair McBean, "Edmund Dell's Manifesto for Mercantilist Liberation," *World Economy* (1986), p. 359. See also R. Michael Gadbaw, "Reciprocity and Its Implications for U.S. Trade Policy," *Journal of Law and Policy in International Business*, vol. 14 (1982), p. 691; and Jagdish Bhagwati and Douglas Irwin, "The Return of the Reciprocitarians—U.S. Trade Policy Today," *World Economy*, vol. 10 (1987), p. 109.

21. See note 2 to chapter 1.

4
The Optional Protocol and
Sector Agreements

The Optional Protocol, or Middle Layer

There are, of course, advantages in trying to obtain somewhat more significant obligations from a core group of like-minded nations to apply to a number of service sectors. Some of those advantages are based on the difficulty of negotiating a significant number of sector agreements and the time it will take to do so. Likewise there may be opportunities for cross-sector swaps (if you agree to include banking, we will agree to include insurance). Consequently there may be room for a set of obligations that would apply to many service sectors. These obligations should very probably specify the sectors to which they apply so as to avoid blank-check worries. The lists of sectors might even become negotiated lists, similar to scheduled tariff concessions in the GATT or the entities in the GATT Government Procurement Code.

The key argument of this paper, however, is that this objective should be accomplished in such a way as not to undermine the establishment of a broadly subscribed legal-institutional structure that will best serve the development of an increasingly significant international discipline for trade in a number of service sectors. This process should take decades.

Thus if more significant obligations are contemplated that might seriously inhibit the adherence of many nations to the structure, it seems wise to put such added obligations into an optional form rather than make them a prerequisite to membership in the umbrella. The obligations might include both some of those listed under the first layer and others listed under the discussion of the sector agreements. For a core group of countries, a negotiating requirement might be that acceptance of the optional protocol is a prerequisite to the coming into force of the whole package of agreements (the umbrella and several sector agreements).

There are several ways to do this, but one that seems efficient is to provide in the umbrella agreement an optional protocol that would specify significant obligations, certainly including a most-favored-nation clause and more impressive regulatory due process and transparency requirements. It might also include a reasonably binding national treatment obligation or principle, but I continue to think that the sectors are sufficiently diverse that details of national treatment and market access obligations will need to be worked out for each sector.

The basic thrust of the optional protocol would be to provide a few obligations for specified sectors. It would also provide that for adherents to the optional protocol that have also accepted a sector agreement, the rules of the sector agreement would prevail over those of the optional protocol. Thus a sector agreement might have an altered or more stringent MFN or national treatment clause, and these would prevail between nations that belong to the sector agreement even if they had accepted the optional protocol. Since the MFN clause in the sector agreement would probably be code conditional, it would be important that the MFN of the optional protocol allow an exception for this kind of clause.

The Nature and Obligations of Sector Agreements

Most substantive international obligations on services trade are likely to be contained in sector agreements, which can be negotiated over a period of decades. A thoughtfully constructed umbrella agreement can furnish both the institutional structure for negotiating and effectively implementing such sector agreements and an incentive for negotiating them. Each agreement can then be tailored to the complex specific needs of a particular sector.

I have already discussed some of the rules and principles for sector agreements. For example, to be approved as an agreement under the umbrella and thus obtain the benefits of such an agreement, including secretariat services, dispute settlement procedures, and certain exemptions from particular general obligations such as MFN, the sector agreement must conform to various umbrella agreement requirements, such as being open to all members of the umbrella agreement. In addition, a sector agreement might contain provisions concerning a long list of topics:

- the extent of a national treatment obligation
- effective market access and its meaning
- subsidies
- dumping

- presence, or questions of the investment (such as the right of establishment) essential for effective delivery of services
- monopoly and competition policies; actions by private firms that damage competition
- the extent to which rules apply to political subdivisions of a federal state
- quantitative versus tariff barriers at government "border" monopolies, state trading, and so on
- government purchases, including the entities covered, standards and technical barriers, transition periods and standstill, and special measures for intellectual property
- safeguards
- grandfather clauses for existing legislation and practices, with provision for phase-out over a period of time
- a committee of signatories; voting, although it might be better to use the umbrella agreement supervisory body with voting restricted to nations that have accepted the sector agreement
- formation and negotiation of new rules and amending the agreement
- supervision of rules and possible provision for complaints or information to be provided by injured private parties, as a procedure leading to the umbrella agreement dispute settlement procedure
- final provisions on ratification, implementation, amending, or reliance on umbrella agreement provisions for these

Each of these topics could be discussed at some length. How obligations on subsidies or dumping, for example, should be applied in specific sectors is a very complex question. Various other study projects, such as that of the services project of the American Enterprise Institute, have explored some of these issues in depth.

5
Conclusion

The necessity of developing an international institutional and rule-oriented framework for discipline on national government measures relating to trade in services is very clear. The time is ripe: the needs are obvious while positions on many issues have not yet hardened into government practices shored up by powerful special interests. Delay could be very damaging since temptations are growing for national governments to cater to domestic service providers at the expense of opportunities for international trade in services. The subject is extremely complex, however. Consequently, a stress on establishing a legal and institutional framework to facilitate a pragmatic, step-by-step evolution of rules for specific service sectors is best. This paper has suggested a number of ways to establish such a framework.

PART TWO

Evaluation and Commentary

Introductory Comments

John S. Reed

The conference agenda today concerns a subject that is important to all of us: trade in services, open markets, and the Uruguay round of negotiations under the General Agreement on Tariffs and Trade (GATT). When we talk about services, we are talking about a part of our economy that is not well understood. Increasingly around the world the development of a service sector is taking on unusual importance within national economies and in international trade. In the United States productivity growth in the service sector will determine the productivity growth in our economy and thus the degree to which our standard of living can be improved. Yet the service sector is ill defined and has not had the attention that it deserves. In international trade, trade in services is even less well understood than either trade in manufactured goods or a service sector within a national economy.

As one of the leading service economies of the world facing severe trade issues, the United States was first to put on the agenda of the GATT the notion that discussions about international trade had to be expanded from the traditional trade in produced goods to include trade in agricultural products and trade in services. Last week in Geneva I saw Ambassador Samuels, the U.S. representative to the talks that are now going on with regard to the Uruguay round. The United States had just tabled a paper stating our position on trade in services. I also talked to a number of ambassadors from other countries and to groups involved in the negotiations, and the consensus was that the Uruguay round is almost destined to succeed. There is little question but that there will be an agreement.

There is another side to the coin. At this point what is evolving is an agreement among professionals and technicians and professional trade negotiators. The private sector, both in the United States and in the countries that constitute our trading partners, is invisible. The negotiations are taking place strictly among professionals. They reflect governmental views, but they do not reflect the views or necessarily enjoy the active support of the private sector.

The developing nations are greatly concerned about the service sectors. They do not understand what is implied by entering into an agreement that touches on the service sector of their economies.

Yet the consensus is that an agreement will be reached. It will be an agreement of great importance in shaping our trade agreements over the next ten or fifteen years because the Uruguay round clearly opens up new fields for agreement. There is thus a real need to have the people who care understand what is going on and to get the results of their understanding built into the positions of the United States and the positions of the other countries engaged in these negotiations.

Finn Caspersen

My role as chairman is not to espouse any particular view. I agree completely with John Reed's observation that the negotiating session is being handled by professionals and is in the government domain. When he was over there, he was the first private sector person that many of the negotiators had talked to. That needs to be remedied, and quickly. If we have an agreement negotiated in a vacuum by governments for governments, it will not augur well for the implementation of the agreement.

My job here is to act as a facilitator. We will first have a statement by Professor John Jackson, whose paper has been distributed to you. Next we will have comments by each of four panelists and then open the session to further comments from the panel and from the audience.

Statement

John H. Jackson

I propose to address this subject in two parts: first, to present a bit of the framework and the background; second, to turn to the potential structure of an agreement—the institutional, legal, or constitutional structure.

I do not come to you as an expert on services or service negotiations. My role is essentially that of a lawyer and, in particular, a lawyer and scholar of the GATT, focusing principally on its institutional structure and that of similar international instruments. It occurred to us this spring that we ought to stop for a moment and think about the institutional structure that might underlie a services agreement and be part of the structure of a services negotiation.

The core idea is that with the growth of service industries worldwide, we are beginning to see risks of partition of markets that are very similar to risks that have occurred in the area of trade in goods for many decades, indeed centuries. Since services seem to be growing so rapidly, a number of governments seem more and more tempted to take actions to segment those markets, to preserve for their domestic interests certain parts of the domestic market. That is a perfectly natural impulse. Governments, after all, are often trying to deliver for their constituents, and they see this as one way to do so: to say that only domestic insurance companies may sell insurance in their territory, or only domestic companies may pursue telecommunications in their territory, and so on. If this situation is left unattended for very long, it may lead to a decrease in world welfare and the welfare of various nations.

There is something to be said for liberal trade concepts based on economic principles, such as comparative advantage, for services, just as there has been for trade in goods. What we need, then, is some kind of international discipline because without it governments are unlikely to liberalize very far. Indeed, there is concern that if one country liberalizes but others do not, the welfare of the liberalizing country may be harmed. Liberalizing is something that must be done in concert. That points to an international discipline, some kind of international rules and obligations. We are all very much aware of the difficulties of making rules that really work, and there has been much criticism about that in the context of the GATT. We cannot say we want a whole loaf or nothing; half a loaf is better than nothing, even though it may not be as good as the whole loaf. Therefore, if we can design a system that will have at least some effect on this process, we are likely to be much better off than without such a system.

We may be strongly tempted to look to the GATT as a model. The question is, Should we have a GATT for services? Or should we bring services into the GATT, the principal instrument for governing international trade in goods? We have launched this process in the context of the eighth trade negotiating round in GATT, the Uruguay round. There has been much conjecture about whether the services rules or framework agreement will be put into the GATT in some way. But just what are we talking about?

The Punta del Este declaration takes a bifurcated approach. A compromise kept the negotiation on services separate from the negotiation on goods and left open the question whether at some point services would be folded into the GATT. As a long-time student and participant and observer of the GATT, I feel some trepidation about using it as a model, because I see all its warts and blemishes. We must recognize, however, that, despite its blemishes, the GATT has been remarkably successful in its forty-year history.

What are the problems of the GATT? I do not want to inventory all of them. Some are laid out in my paper. I want to mention a few salient ones to indicate the source of some of my worries.

It has sometimes been asked whether we could simply amend the GATT to include services. Wherever the GATT mentions goods or products, we might simply add "and services." I think that approach would be fatal, and I do not think that is what governments intend or what anyone has been advocating.

It would be a damaging approach for at least two reasons. First, many of the rules of GATT do not easily apply to services. We would be forcing into those rules a new subject matter that would not fit. It would stretch those rules, it would cause them to be misapplied, or it would create an ambiguity that would allow governments to squirm out of their obligations.

Moreover, the GATT is very hard to amend. This is one of the problems that stem from its history. The GATT amending process is such that most people feel that it is virtually impossible to amend. The membership, which started with twenty-two countries forty years ago, is now ninety-five and growing fast. The minimum amending requirement is a two-thirds vote, and parts require unanimity to amend. Since unanimity has never been obtained for an amendment to the GATT, that really is not a useful course. Even two-thirds would require conceding a series of negotiating points to a large body of countries that may not have much interest in a services negotiation.

Even if we do not bring services into the GATT, we might design a new agreement with GATT as the model. But there are some potential dangers there too.

First, the GATT was never intended to be what it is today. It was designed as a reciprocal agreement for the reduction of tariffs and was supposed to be tended to by an International Trade Organization (ITO). But that organization never came into being, and the GATT has had to subsist and indeed to move to fill the vacuum.

Because of that history the GATT's institutional structure is very weak. I have mentioned the amending problem. The GATT has enormous problems with respect to decision making and rule making, or the development of new obligations. As a consequence, in the Tokyo round the tendency was to move outside the GATT and to develop side codes for various purposes. The dispute settlement procedure also has problems.

What we should do, then, is to think anew about an advisable constitutional framework for international trade in services. Several core points that I would like to make may be the basis of some of our discussion.

First, we ought to realize that we are making a constitution. That is, we are embarked on a long-range affair. Expertise and knowledge about the service industries are very skimpy, and it seems implausible that within a very few years, even within the span of the Uruguay round, we will develop any full-blown, fully finished agreement on services.

We must set in place a framework for the evolution of a full-blown system that will occur over many decades. There are some models for that procedure, such as the government procurement code idea in the Tokyo round. That code sacrificed breadth and coverage to set up a framework that could evolve. We should be thinking about a framework that will enable this process to continue for many years in the light of new study and of new sectors that may arise.

A core point ought to be as wide a participation as possible. Of course, a few countries, such as the countries of the Organization for Economic Cooperation and Development, might go off in a corner and negotiate something that they were reasonably satisfied with and implement it. But such a procedure might be to the detriment of the rest of the world and of the initial participants since other countries might not be willing to be drawn into the process of developing disciplines that they would accept. The history of GATT illustrates this. The developing countries did not like the GATT at the outset. Many do not like it today.

Any framework that we design should have some portion that would have a broad membership—developing, undeveloped, and industrial countries, perhaps even nonmarket economies. The aim should be to get them involved in developing information about the sectors, concepts of transparency and publication of rules, and some of the other soft ideas of obligation.

What might be the legal framework of such an agreement? We probably must have at least a two-level structure. At the first level would be an umbrella agreement on trade in services that would set out the framework.

We would leave to a second level particular sector agreements, which would evolve. Initially there might be only several such agreements, but we would allow for more to be entered into, carrying us well into the next century.

What should be in each of these levels? Are two levels enough?

The essential question at the outset, then, is how to set up the umbrella agreement. An agreement that has many stringent obligations, though pragmatically very appealing, will lose breadth of membership. The stronger the initial obligations in the umbrella agreement, the harder it will be to attract a broad membership.

Consequently, we need to tailor the umbrella agreement to a broad membership. It might, however, include obligations that, although they sound soft, are quite meaningful. We might, for example, set up a centralized structure for dispute settlement that would avoid some of the defects of the GATT system. Transparency requirements might also be useful. Furthermore, we need an institutional or decision-making structure. There we must think ahead. It will be very hard to manage a meaningful organization with a broad membership that is based on a one-nation, one-vote system. The structure should also include rules about how specific sector agreements are to be negotiated and how they will relate to the umbrella agreement.

One difficult issue is the question of most-favored-nation treatment, and another is the question of national treatment. If we follow the analogy of GATT, we would include both of these in the new structure for services. But there are some substantial risks in blindly following that analogy.

The most-favored-nation principle has some important policy arguments in its favor, but it also has some risks, among them the so-called foot-dragger, or least common denominator, problem. If every obligation in an umbrella agreement must be applied to every member of the organization unconditionally, many countries will lack the incentive to enhance the discipline of the system; they will say, "We can stay out while the others go ahead; whatever they do will benefit us without our having to pay for it." The foot-dragger problem brings up issues of how to adjust the most-favored-nation clause toward code conditionality; that is, the clause would apply to those countries prepared to accept certain obligations, such as a sector code or some kind of intermediate layer that would be somewhat more stringent than membership in the framework agreement.

The other obligation that has often been talked about is national treatment, the notion that countries must treat foreign providers just as they treat domestic providers of services or goods. That is the core obligation of this process. Some have suggested that we need a national treatment obligation in an umbrella agreement that would apply to all services or all service sectors.

It is hard to see how a generalized national treatment clause would work. It would become riddled with exceptions, and it would be evaded. I also doubt that many countries would want to sign such a blank check as a national treatment obligation that would apply to future and unknown service sectors. Perhaps in the umbrella national treatment should be simply a statement of principle and not a binding obligation. Then we would leave the details to the service sector agreements.

Commentary

Geza Feketekuty

The main focus of our attention should be what goes into the framework agreement. The Uruguay Declaration provides remarkable guidance on the negotiations on trade in services and the framework agreement. It says that the negotiations should aim to establish a multilateral framework of principles and rules for trade in services, including the elaboration of possible disciplines for individual sectors. The stated objective is to achieve an expansion of trade in services under conditions of transparency and progressive liberalization.

What does this mean? First, it means that the framework agreement developed in these negotiations should contain some general principles and rules applicable to all services and more detailed rules geared to specific sectors. The second sentence says that the purpose of establishing general rules and principles is to expand trade and that this should be achieved by making barriers visible and establishing a process for gradually getting rid of them.

The declaration goes on to state that the negotiations "shall respect the policy objectives of national laws and regulations." Most barriers to trade in services are embedded in domestic regulations. A framework must therefore enable us to sort out what is a barrier and what is a domestic regulation. This will not be easy since many policy measures that a foreign exporting country sees as a trade barrier the importing country will see as a legitimate form of domestic regulation.

Third, the framework must spell out the rights and obligations of countries that agree to subscribe to the framework and participate in the negotiated reduction of barriers. While the need for a statement of rights and obligations is not explicitly mentioned in the Uruguay Declaration, it is implied.

In summary, the framework developed in the negotiations needs to be both a constitution for world trade in services and a negotiator's tool kit.

Now let us look at the elements of the framework agreement in more detail. First, I agree with John Jackson that it should contain a clear statement of objectives and that such a statement of objectives needs to emphasize the liberalization aspect. Second, the framework needs to establish rules that spell out the negotiating procedures and the nature of the commitments that are to be negotiated. I would go further than Jackson in spelling out a menu of negotiating commitments that negotiators could use in subsequent negotiations. Finally, I agree with Jackson that the framework must clearly define the legal rights and obligations of the participants.

This brings me to the critical question posed by Jackson, namely, whether we should include any substantive obligations in the framework. I agree with Jackson that the framework itself should not contain binding obligations to remove barriers to trade in services. It should lay out negotiating procedures for doing so, however, and I would negotiate a separate package of liberalization measures that would be implemented at the same time that the framework is adopted.

The bilateral agreements the United States has negotiated on trade in services with Israel and Canada provide two possible models for a framework agreement in the GATT. The agreement with Israel applies the general rules of the framework agreement to all transborder trade in services on a best efforts basis. In addition, Israel and the United States committed themselves to a sector-by-sector review of the regulations that affect trade in services and the development of binding commitments. Over the past few years we have reviewed the regulatory measures that affect trade in tourism, in insurance, and in telecommunications, data processing, and information services; and we have developed sectoral annotations of the general principles and concepts contained in the umbrella agreement. These sectoral annotations are expected to form the basis for a legally binding document.

The agreement we negotiated with Canada offers a different model. The general rules of the framework agreement with Israel are legally binding, but they apply only to new measures and regulations. All existing regulations that are inconsistent with the rules of the agreement are grandfathered. The agreement establishes a negotiating process for removing trade barriers embedded in current regulations.

In addition to the general framework, the U.S.-Canadian agreement contains a number of sectoral understandings. An agreement on enhanced telecommunications services in effect extends the relatively unregulated environment that now exists in each country to trade between the two countries. An agreement on architecture builds on negotiations carried out between the National Institute for

Architectural Review Boards in the United States and the relevant bodies in the Canadian provinces, which have focused on the establishment of agreed principles and procedures for qualifying architects from the other country. An agreement on tourism services establishes a basis for open trade in services sold to tourists.

Neither the Israeli nor the Canadian framework agreement on trade in services establishes any binding obligations to remove existing barriers to trade. The Israeli agreement builds on a best efforts commitment; the Canadian agreement grandfathers existing regulations inconsistent with the free trade principles built into the framework. It remains to be seen which of these two approaches is adopted in a multilateral framework agreement. Each approach has advantages and disadvantages.

This brings me to the really tough question: How do we separate trade barriers from legitimate domestic regulations? One possible test would be to examine whether a regulation explicitly discriminates against foreign suppliers of a particular service. One might create a presumption that any measure that treats domestic suppliers one way and foreign suppliers another way is a barrier. In other words, any measure that does not give foreigners national treatment could be considered a barrier.

A national treatment test is not a perfect test for the existence of barriers, however. Many measures that meet the national treatment test nevertheless create barriers to trade. Any regulation, for example, that limits the total number of firms authorized to sell particular services could create a barrier to trade, even if the same ceiling applies to both domestic and foreign firms. Assume a government is willing to license only ten firms to provide insurance and that all ten licenses have been issued to domestic firms. No foreign firm will be able to sell insurance, even though the regulation does not on its face discriminate against foreigners.

Regulations that limit innovation can also create major barriers to trade, even though no overt discrimination against foreigners is involved. Why does such a regulation create a trade barrier? It is a trade barrier because the ability of a foreign company to penetrate a new market tends to depend on its ability to innovate, particularly where prices are also determined by the regulators. A foreign company entering a new market needs some kind of economic edge, and that edge is frequently provided by new technology or the development of new products.

One recent example involved a country that regulates not only the premium charged by insurance companies for various types of risk but also the types of risk that insurance companies are allowed to insure against. An American insurance company in this country had the idea of insuring suppliers of telephone poles against future liability claims. In this country the telephone company makes suppliers pay for the replacement of poles that develop cracks. Before the American insurance company could offer a new kind of policy insuring suppliers of telephone poles against the risk of such poles developing cracks, it had to obtain permission from the regulatory authorities. The regulators, however, thought that this new idea needed extensive study and analysis, and the business opportunity was lost.

How do we deal with these kinds of regulations without getting into a detailed negotiation over the substance of domestic regulations, something the Uruguay Declaration said should not be done? In any case, any effort to harmonize national regulations would be extremely time consuming and would result in very long and complex negotiations. Switzerland and the European Community have negotiated an 800-page agreement on insurance that addresses every possible regulatory situation. It took ten years to negotiate and almost as long to explain to the legislatures. It is obviously impossible for eighty countries to pursue the same kind of approach. We therefore have to develop an approach that sets some basic ground rules and procedures for sorting out issues as they arise.

I cannot offer a detailed blueprint at this time, but let me review the desirable characteristics of a framework agreement. We want an agreement that will encompass a large number of countries, that will encompass a large number of sectors, that will provide substantial liberalization, that will give early concrete results, and that will result in clear and precise understandings and commitments so as to prevent future conflict and confusion.

We cannot achieve all these things to the same degree, and we will therefore have to decide how much weight to give to each. The whole debate at this point is about the trade-offs that have to be made among these objectives in designing a negotiating process. That is the central challenge we face.

How do we design a structure in which to make these trade-offs? What are the trade-offs in the real world? To what extent must we give up one objective for another? These are factual questions that are difficult to define in the abstract because they depend on so many different factors that will become apparent only in the course of the negotiations. Let me make a few obvious points about these trade-offs.

First, if we want early results, we must devise either a system in which we get results in a few areas first or a system in which we initially get broad, vague results. We could also devise an approach in which we get a handful of concrete results and some broad rules that cover most sectors. Both the Israeli and the Canadian agreements are instructive in this respect.

Second, we can choose between very substantial liberalization among a small group of countries or lesser liberalization among a much broader group of countries. Alternatively we could devise a system that will give us some of both. We could combine a shallow agreement with limited obligations that will encompass many countries with procedures that would allow some countries to go much further among themselves. Similarly, we can choose between substantial liberalization in a few sectors, lesser liberalization of the full range of sectors, or some of both. In other words, we can have some general rules that do not create very substantial obligations and add to them more detailed rules for specific sectors that would establish more far-reaching obligations.

In confronting these trade-offs, I would suggest some basic ground rules. One is that we must maintain a constant balance and tension between the broad liberalization objectives reflected in general trade principles and the realism that can only be provided by a more sectoral focus to rule making. In other words, we have to be realistic enough to recognize that we cannot remove barriers to trade embedded in regulations without addressing the sectoral, regulatory issues but not so realistic that we lose sight of the liberalization objective and the broad trade principles of an umbrella agreement. One thing I worry about is how we can keep any sectoral negotiations from coming under the complete control of the regulators, who are more interested in preserving their regulations than in advancing the liberalization of trade.

A second ground rule I would like to suggest is that we should be clear about the legal character of the commitments that are negotiated. We can negotiate either vague political commitments or precise legal commitments, but in either case we should be very clear about their character. Legal commitments should be precise and clear. If we negotiate something more generic and ambiguous, we should describe it as a political commitment rather than a legal obligation.

A third ground rule I would make is that we should aim for some early concrete liberalization measures, even if only in a few limited areas. At the same time we should aim for the development of general rules that cover all services, even if that means that such general rules end up being less far reaching. We should aim to establish a general framework that covers all service sectors, but at the same time we should find a way to negotiate simultaneously an initial package of liberalization measures.

The fourth ground rule I would establish is that we should keep as many countries in the game as we can but at the same time devise a system whereby those countries that want to go further in limiting the flexibility of regulators to restrict access to one another's markets can do so.

Claude E. Barfield

I would like to start with something that Finn Caspersen said—that one of the problems we face in this negotiation is that it is highly technical and hard to mobilize support for.

First let me make two points about the current trade bill that bring the service negotiations to the here and now. Those interested in services should be very much interested in several elements of the trade bill, specifically the principle of bilateral reciprocity that the Gephardt amendment attempts to enshrine in U.S. law. Both the Gephardt amendment and the so-called compromise that Dan Rostenkowski and others worked out put into U.S. law a principle that no economist of any stripe would agree with: that the running of a bilateral surplus with another nation over a period of time is prima facie evidence of unfair trade practices.

Remember that from the middle to the late 1970s our trade surplus was carried by services on the one hand and by high-technology goods and services on the other. In the 1990s, if we pass some form of bilateral reciprocity, it is services that will be affected because trade in services is one of the areas with high-technology goods in which we are likely to go back into surplus with other nations and regions.

Second, the attempt of Congress to tie the president's hands in relation to the GATT negotiations will be deleterious not only to services but to the entire negotiations. We are not sure how that will come out, but there seems to have been some movement to have the president come back for small slices, to have Congress get into more and more detail. One of the things that trade negotiators do not like to point out is the dirty little secret that Yes, there are going to be trade-offs in the GATT negotiations.

There will be trade-offs between services and other areas—agriculture, basic industries, intellectual property. For what we get we will have to give some things.

There will also be trade-offs within the services area. No one in this room knows what those will be. But the wider the latitude we give the negotiators, the better opportunity we have for an equitable agreement. The more times they have to come back, not only in the United States but in other countries, to their individual representative bodies, the less opportunity we have for wide-ranging and necessary breakthroughs in the Uruguay round.

John Jackson and Geza Feketekuty and others like them over the past year or so have pulled back in relation to what they think is possible in a so-called umbrella or framework agreement. They have more and more focused on the idea that the real negotiation will be in the sectors.

I would like to present another potential model. Jackson's paper is an excellent end position, that is, a statement of where we would like to be at the end of negotiations. But I would like to start the negotiations by attempting a little more. That is, we might freight the umbrella agreement with a number of the principles that we have talked about: nondiscrimination, transparency, national treatment, most-favored-nation treatment. At the outset nations that agree to this should be allowed to stipulate exceptions, to state where their particular regulatory systems cannot be reconciled. Those exceptions should be only for a stated period. That is, along with a framework or an umbrella agreement, we negotiate a schedule according to which individual nations work toward legal compliance with those principles.

Another thing we ought to think about—in the umbrella agreement and possibly in the sector agreements—is limiting the sectors. That is, the GATT negotiators in their initial negotiations should lay out what the major traded sectors are. This may or may not work, but it is a way to limit the universe and to limit the nervousness of nations in signing a document when they do not know exactly what kind of new service might come into being for which they would be legally bound to GATT rules.

The model I have suggested as an alternative would have a fairly strong umbrella agreement with the kinds of exceptions that I mention. I also think that any model should include what a couple of years ago was called GATT plus and Jackson has called an optional alternative. Such a provision would allow nations that wanted to go beyond whatever is agreed on to get together on a conditional most-favored-nation basis.

How does the proposal that the United States put on the table in early November, which is our opening shot for the service negotiations, square with what we have been talking about here? The language seems to be a throwback to discussions of a year ago about the trade-offs between the right of establishment on the one hand and the right of market access on the other. What this document lays out is a set of rights and obligations in relation to market access. In discussing national treatment, it says that the kinds of principles that should be put into effect are access to local distribution networks, access to local firms and personnel, access to customers, access to licenses, and the right to use brand names. There has not been much discussion of those kinds of principles in the past year or so.

Another way of looking at the negotiations is as negotiations between competing regulatory systems—the way we organize our banking system vis-à-vis the way the Canadians or the French do. How can we reconcile those differences? We have begun to think out logistically under what conditions and what rules we lock in our domestic regulators, which are in some cases increasingly also international regulators, with our trade negotiators.

Those of you interested in particular sectors know that you suddenly see that the Federal Communications Commission has created a rule, or is thinking about a rule, that you might have thought would be the business of the trade negotiators. The trade negotiators are probably encroaching on places that the FCC and other regulatory agencies think are theirs. We have not thought out in this country or any other country how those two systems are geared together.

Jackson set out as a theme of his paper the necessity to move from what he called power-oriented negotiations to rule-oriented negotiations. He suggests that when a future panel of the GATT makes a decision in relation to a sector or an alleged infringement, that decision go back to the supervisory body so that we get a political judgment on it.

I agree that we have to look at the political realities. But it ought to be made quite difficult for the services body in GATT to overturn a panel's decision. A majority vote should not be sufficient; 60 percent or two-thirds should be required to overturn a panel's vote, which is the most insulated from political pressures.

Finally, it seems to me absolutely necessary that the existing GATT secretariat also be the secretariat for services. We do not need competing bureaucracies in Geneva. They must report to the same person.

Richard R. Rivers

John Jackson has written an admirable paper on a difficult subject, one that is not easy to define or structure. If this were the end of the Uruguay trade negotiation, Jackson's paper were on the table, and I were the U.S. negotiator, I would grab it. Regrettably, it is not the end but the beginning of the Uruguay round. I am concerned that the paper concedes too much.

Ten years ago the U.S. government sent me to London to negotiate with the British government on what must have been the first bilateral services negotiation. It had to do with the screen time quota that the British government imposed on BBC broadcasting. It limited programming of U.S. origin to ninety minutes a day. We raised this issue with the British government in a timid way. By the time we were finished and the British Screen Actors Guild had got through with it and we had brought it to their attention, the quota had been shrunk from ninety minutes to sixty minutes a day. They thought it was altogether too liberal.

My message is that we need to be bold. It is commonplace in this city to hear people say that the GATT does not work and is a failure and ought to be scrapped. Like so many commonplace statements, that one is about 90 percent wrong. The people who make it reveal how ignorant they are of the past fifty years of human history.

The fact is that the GATT, in many areas, has been a spectacular success. It accomplished its central objective, which was the negotiated reciprocal reduction of tariffs under a system of bindings. In many other ways it has been a spectacular success through which all of us have benefited. That is not a very popular thing to say in this city today. The GATT is not a perfect document either. We all know it is very imperfect. But its imperfections lie in the areas in which people were timid in 1947, such as agriculture. The failure of the United States to strike while the iron was hot in 1947 makes the GATT rules on agriculture so pitiful today. Again, the GATT dispute settlement rules worked for a while, but the governments recoiled from doing anything to address that very delicate and specific area. So I would caution against timidity, although I recognize the intricacies and the difficulties of negotiating in this area.

I like the structure that Jackson has outlined. We need an umbrella agreement. Some GATT principles such as nondiscrimination may have more application to services than we might think at first glance. But we need an evolutionary and organic international agreement regulating services that will spin off sectoral agreements tailored to the sectors' particular needs. I agree that in the umbrella agreement many of these obligations ought to be selective. We are really talking about a kind of GATT general agreement on trade in services a la carte.

We should not approach this timidly. It would be a pity if the Uruguay round produced an agreement in the nature of an OECD declaration and some hortatory language about tourism. I do not want that to happen. This subject is too important to allow that to be the result.

We must be ambitious. I agree with Geza Feketekuty that there are trade-offs in this negotiation; that is inherent in a negotiation. We cannot have all the liberalization we want. We cannot necessarily combine that with the breadth of membership and the participation that we would like. We cannot include all the sectors at the outset, and we cannot do it overnight. We cannot have early results.

We need to be aggressive and bold and ambitious. We need as much liberalization as we can accomplish. We should not let the foot draggers hold us back. We cannot let this subject also be reduced to the lowest common denominator.

Let us have broad membership; let us have as many people as possible sign the broad agreement. But to the extent that they are unwilling to go along, so be it; they may change their minds later.

Joan Spero

First, John Jackson has made a very important contribution. He has contributed to what I would call the missing link. That is, we have spent a lot of time talking about an umbrella agreement and looking at what should be included in various sectoral agreements. But we have not spent much time talking about how we get from here to there—what, as Jackson says, the constitutional elements might be or what Geza Feketekuty has described as the nature of the process that would be embedded in the agreement.

A number of us here were involved several years ago in making a first stab at what a services agreement should be like. We came up with a paper based on an ideal model. It would have had a number of substantive binding principles in an umbrella agreement. Those principles would have covered a large number of sectors, either directly or through negotiation of subagreements. The services agreement would not just have included a standstill but would have rolled back many existing services restrictions through the sectoral agreements. It would have had a large number of signatories, both for the umbrella and for the sectoral agreements.

The problem we face is the political reality and the possibility of achieving these things at home or outside the United States, where the receptivity to a services agreement is mixed. The question is, Given those constraints, what is a second-best alternative? What is the balance between the rigor of an agreement and the membership that we want in that agreement?

Jackson makes a very important contribution in talking about the constitutional element, the framework for the continuing process of liberalizing services trade. Let me raise a couple of questions about that.

The first concerns where to make the trade-off between rigor and breadth. When do we make it? Do we make it now? Do we really want an umbrella agreement that is nonbinding, with very few obligations, to which many nations would subscribe? Or do we prefer a tougher, more substantive, and binding umbrella agreement to which perhaps just a few like-minded nations would subscribe?

Now is not the time to make that decision. We may have a fairly positive model on the table in the United States–Canada agreement. Certainly those two nations are about as like-minded as you can get. We are now debating the issue of where we expect to end up and where we start.

Another question I have about the Jackson paper is the complexity of the system he lays out. Having spent some time at the United Nations, I am concerned about different levels of participation, about the ability to achieve meaningful distribution of voting rights and the like. I recognize that he has not tackled that head on.

If we are thinking about a supervisory body, how could we make that institution as active as possible? How could we give it powers to take the initiative in identifying barriers to services trade and promoting further services negotiations?

Another question is how to avoid rigidities in the system. We can spend all our time negotiating this constitution and debating voting rights and then find that the system will have a veto over continuing negotiation.

On the need to harmonize regulation and the impossibility of doing so, the European Economic Community (EEC) is now engaged in a negotiation to create an internal market, supposedly by 1992. One of their techniques is not to try to harmonize regulation with 800 pages of agreement but to rely on home country regulation, to set certain minimum standards, and to look to the home country regulator to meet those standards. Perhaps this is a model that we could look to.

A final point is more an observation about the political environment that goes back to the question of who is going to sign this agreement. Many of us wonder whether this will be a developed country agreement, an OECD agreement, or an agreement that includes the developing countries. That seems to be where the break comes.

A broader concern to my mind is not the developing countries or even Japan but rather the EEC. Many of us in the United States assume that the EEC is on board in this exercise, and I think that is generally true. But I see some trends in the EEC that I will put on the table.

Although a number of governments and participants in the private sector in the EEC are very committed and interested in trade in services, another train leaving the station is a potential distraction to that effort. That is the question of the internal market. The internal market, which would involve a number of service sectors, such as transportation and financial services, can be a positive development in liberalizing trade in services within Europe. At the same time the preoccupation with the internal market may well distract the Europeans from a focus on the GATT. As we learned in the negotiations with Canada, one can keep only so many balls in the air at the same time.

Second, a more troubling possibility is a feeling among some participants in the EEC that they cannot negotiate in the GATT until they get their own house in order, that they must get their internal market organized before they are willing to negotiate with others. It is thus very important in this process to focus not only on how to keep the less-developed countries involved but also on how to keep Europe involved.

Discussion

PROFESSOR JACKSON: One point I would like to respond to is whether this is a starting point for a negotiation or an ending point, whether it is ambitious or too cautious. I do not think the issue comes out so neatly. This paper is extremely ambitious in many ways with respect to constitution making—much more ambitious than many negotiators would like to think about. Quite often negotiators like not to think about constitution making. They like to avoid issues that they think are only for the far distant future. They would just as soon get on with the deal making that is now going on.

I think that is very dangerous. We had it in the GATT. The GATT has served us very well, much better than we had a right to expect. But some of its problems have arisen because of the failure of the ITO and the failure of the process back in the 1940s.

The GATT is extremely complex now. It has a number of side agreements. There are some tough legal issues, which give governments ways to weasel out of obligations. The legal issues concern how the various codes relate to the GATT.

What does the most-favored-nation principle, for instance, mean in connection with some of the codes? Part of what I am saying in this paper is that we must try to avoid the errors of the past and to take the history and the experience of the GATT into account in doing so.

My paper presents the structure of a potentially very strong first offer. I have reinforced the concept of the middle layer. The structure is one of an umbrella agreement on the one hand and a series of sector agreements on the other. But I suggest an optional protocol in the umbrella agreement, as in some other treaties, particularly in the human rights area. In certain other dispute settlement areas we have treaties with optional protocols whereby some governments can accept only the basic treaty while others accept higher obligations.

The optional protocol should probably include stringent obligations as a starting point for a negotiation. But the framework agreement could be accepted by countries not yet at a stage where they could accept many stringent obligations. That way we would get everybody into the process and get the key players thinking about a much higher level of discipline.

All of this will be affected by the negotiating context. And Geza Feketekuty is absolutely right. There must be trade-offs. Right now, we do not have in our minds a scale of priorities for some of these principles. Those will begin to harden and develop as the negotiation goes on and we discover more facts. We have to understand all that, and there will be accommodation.

It is not too early to begin thinking about the policies behind some of those trade-offs that we see coming in a few years. One of those trade-offs is whether we are trying for a tiny group of nations with a high amount of discipline or for a very broad group of nations with subgroups committed to a much higher discipline.

We may not need to have a trade-off. We may be able to eat our cake and have it too if the different layers are understood and work together appropriately. Of course, that will mean complexity but less complexity than we now have in the GATT, which is not only complex but ambiguous around the borders between the various agreements and provisions.

MR. CASPERSEN: Claude Barfield raised the question of exactly how the comments today and Professor Jackson's paper square with the proposal that is now on the table in the negotiations. Mr. Barfield, would you like to elaborate on that?

MR. BARFIELD: It seems to me that the language in the details of the U.S. position is a throwback to the discussions and the internal position of the U.S. trade representative about a year and a half ago. There was a great deal of concern then about the trade-offs between the right of establishment on the one hand and the so-called right of market access on the other.

MR. RIVERS: My reaction to the U.S. proposal is that it bears the imprint of material that is not well thought through. That is all right; at this point a lot of things are not well thought through. It has already provoked considerable reaction, and what we want at this time is that kind of thinking and reaction. But I do not see enough sensitivity to some of the issues that we have been discussing.

MR. FEKETEKUTY: We started by trying to put together what an ideal agreement would look like, by setting out a vision of what we are trying to do in this agreement. In a negotiating process we must find out exactly how much we can accomplish in each substantive area. We have set out the limits, and we must see what compromises emerge. Once we see how far we can push the various principles, what kind of

a negotiating procedure we can establish to apply substantive obligations in these various areas, we can then decide how to build a
constitution.

PROFESSOR JACKSON: That is what worries me. We saw this a bit in the
Tokyo round. There was a conflict about whether we should try to
reform the dispute settlement process and unify it early in the negotiation or leave that to the end after the substance was negotiated.

It is a circular question. It is a chicken-and-egg or dog-chasing-its-
tail question, because the nature of the constitution affects what
nations are willing to accept as obligations. The obligations have a
meaning only in the context of the legal framework. To leave all of this
to the end may foreclose certain of the options that we might well
want to consider at the beginning.

MR. FEKETEKUTY: What do you mean by the end? It certainly has to be
done before we come up with a piece of paper that looks like print-
ing—

PROFESSOR JACKSON: If by the end, you mean next summer, fine.

MS. SPERO: I don't know if we will be able to work out the voting
arrangements in the right way or if this is exactly the constitution we
want. But I think there is a missing link in the way at least we in the
private sector have been thinking about what the thing would look
like. I would be interested to know what the conversation has been
now that that paper is down. People will say, exactly what is it that we
are signing on to with this paper? What do we mean? Are we going to
be signing on to a standstill? Are we going to sign something that will
be binding on us? So I think that John Jackson has raised a very
important point. We must begin to think about the process and what
the institutions will look like. Among the hard questions is how to get
around the issue of right of establishment. Can we redefine the right
of establishment as we tried to do with the right of market access? The
paper that the United States has put down does not talk about the
right of establishment, but it tries to define it in a variety of ways. That
is going to be one of the gut issues.

PROFESSOR JACKSON: A negotiation that aims to eliminate discrimination is probably much simpler than a negotiation that aims to eliminate discriminatory effects, and that would be much simpler than a
negotiation that seeks to deal with the problems that an American

business office struggles with—regulations that prevent innovation, introduction of new technology, greater degrees of competition, deregulation. We need to set our sights on what we are trying to do. Are we just trying to eliminate open discrimination, are we trying to eliminate discriminatory effects, or are we trying to eliminate elements of the regulations that prevent innovation and competition? That is one of the issues we have not yet confronted.

Second, on Barfield's point about the relationship between trade negotiators and regulators, we have not gone very far in our country. We are struggling in the Canadian negotiation with how to define some of the elements or some of the terms that we use.

The trade negotiators are saying that we must define some of these terms, and the regulators are telling us that would prejudge future regulations. People do not yet understand the difference between a trade agreement and a domestic regulatory process or exactly how the two relate to each other. That is something we have not sorted out in U.S. law or even conceptually.

RICHARD SNAPE (World Bank): I think it is probably not fair to say that the paper is premature. It was, after all, not a U.S. negotiating position but a paper saying what might happen.

I have four points. One is on the most-favored-nation principle and the point that was made about foot dragging or free riding. What was not mentioned was the other side of it, the constraint that non-discrimination puts on members once the agreement has been made—that they may not do to anyone what they are not prepared to do to their best friend.

If we think of how protection has increased through nontariff barriers, they have all been discriminatory. I think Professor Jackson gives away too much and that there should be an attempt, despite foot dragging and free riding, to extend the most-favored-nation principle as broadly as possible.

Second is the question of national treatment. National treatment in the GATT, of course, says that, once across the frontier, things will be treated equally. But what is the frontier in services? Perhaps that is focused on a bit too much, because another way of looking at national treatment under the GATT is to say that once you have crossed a legitimate barrier, you will be treated exactly as the nationals are treated. The legitimate barrier in the GATT is the tariff.

The way to go with the umbrella agreement would be to say there would be no discrimination against foreigners except as any sector agreement legitimizes a particular barrier or constraint. There would be a presumption of complete equality of treatment. The onus would be on each sector agreement to legitimize a particular barrier, and no other barriers would be permitted.

Third, a criterion that should be specified for sector agreements is that they be liberalizing. That may be obvious, but it was not mentioned. Why is it important? The sector agreements that have been made within the broad umbrella of GATT so far have all been non-liberalizing—the multifiber arrangement and the codes for meats and dairy products.

The risk is always that sector agreements will be not liberalizing; it is not trivial to make it a criterion for a sector agreement that it be judged to be liberalizing—not more liberal than some alternative worse scenario but more liberal than the status quo.

Fourth, how does a country join sector agreements? We have a very bad precedent in the subsidies code. Even though countries sign the subsidies code and believe that they have agreed to its conditions, the United States has independently said that it will not accept those people as members unless they satisfy U.S. conditions. The club rules should be judged corporately, not separately by each individual member.

JOSEPH GREENWALD (former negotiator in the GATT): The Canadian agreement is touted as a model for the GATT. Does that mean we are moving toward a grandfathered services agreement?

MR. FEKETEKUTY: I don't think we have decided that issue.

MR. GREENWALD: So it is not the model?

MR. FEKETEKUTY: I think it is one of the models.

QUESTION: We know that there are many links between goods and services—services including goods, goods including services. How can we devise a frame for the rules for services without defining the borderline within GATT between the goods agreement and the services?

MR. FEKETEKUTY: One approach is that anything not covered in the GATT will be covered in the new agreement. But then what do we do about things like films? The GATT has some rules about motion pictures, but one could also argue that they fit into the services area. We will just have to sort those things out.

We also have the problem in semiconductor chips. At what point are we talking about intellectual property or a service, and at what point are we talking about a product? We have had a GATT panel on this very issue. The GATT said that when a product contains an intellectual value that far exceeds the value of the material product, the GATT rules ought to apply strictly to the material product. That is something we will have to struggle with.

MURRAY SMITH (Institute for Research on Public Policy in Canada): I have a question for John Jackson. I have shared for many years his preference for a rules-based system over a power-based system. I would like him to elaborate on what he is suggesting for dispute settlement. The two paragraphs in the paper on those issues seem to point toward the kinds of proposals he made in the late 1970s for a much more formal dispute settlement process than exists in the GATT.

PROFESSOR JACKSON: I think that is fair. Some of those paragraphs are taken verbatim from an earlier article. I wanted to remind the reader of these premises. I don't know whether it is much more formal than the current GATT process, because that process has become reasonably formal. I do think some additional things are needed.

Index

Agriculture sector, 9, 56
Airline industry, 10
Antidumping duties, 8
Architecture agreement, 49–50

Balance-of-payments problems, 8, 14 n.28
Banking industry, 10, 16, 17
Barfield, Claude E., 53–55, 61
Brazil, 33 n.18
Bretton Woods Agreement Act of 1945, 18

Canada–United States free trade pact, 29, 49–50, 64
Caspersen, Finn, 42, 61
Comparative advantage, 4
Consultation obligation, 25
Contracting parties, 7
Countervailing duties, 8
Cuba, 13–14 n.27
Customs unions, 9, 29
Czechoslovakia, 13–14 n.27

Developing countries, 30–31, 42, 46
Dispute settlement, 17, 23–24, 36, 46, 56, 60, 65
Due process obligations, 8, 25, 35
Dumping issues, 35

Economic development exceptions, 9
EEC. See European Economic Community
Embargo use, 13 n.27
Employment rules, 16
Engineering services, 10
Escape clauses, 9, 30
Establishment, right of, 16, 36, 54, 61, 62
European Economic Community (EEC), 51, 58–59
Exemptions and exceptions, 8–9, 29–30

Federal Communications Commission, 55
Feketekuty, Geza, 48–53, 61–62, 64–65

Final clauses, 22, 31, 36
Foreign Assistance Act of 1963, 13–14 n.27
Foreign investment protection, 16
France, 12 n.3
Free Trade Agreement between the United States and Canada, 29, 49–50, 64
Free trade areas, 9, 29

General Agreement on Tariffs and Trade (GATT)
    amendment process, 15, 44–45
    assessment of, 9–10, 45, 56, 60
    core obligations, 8
    dispute settlement, 23, 56
    due process, 8, 25
    exemptions and exceptions, 8–9, 29–30
    inapplicability to service trale, 15–16, 44–45
    membership, 9
    as model for services agreement, 4, 5, 44, 45
    most-favored-nation provisions, 8, 11, 27, 32 n.4
    negotiations process, 53–54
    purpose, 7–8, 45
    services agreement, relationship to, 21, 55
    U.S. law, relationship to, 8, 18
    waiver provisions, 30
General services protocol, 17. See also Optional protocol
Gephardt amendment, 53
Germany, Federal Republic of (West), 12 n.3
Grandfather exceptions, 9, 36, 64
Greenwald, Joseph, 64
Gross national product, service trade percentage, 3

Health and welfare exception, 9, 29
Human rights policy, 60

IMF. *See* International Monetary Fund
India, 33 n.18
Industrial policies, 9
Insurance industry, 10, 17, 50–51
Intellectual property, 9, 29, 65
International Chamber of Commerce, 11 n.2
International Civil Aviation Organization, 11 n.2, 31
International Emergency Economic Powers Act, 13–14 n.27
International Labor Office, 11 n.2
International Maritime Organization, 11 n.2, 31
International Monetary Fund (IMF), 7, 18, 21
International Telecommunications Union, 11 n.2, 31
International Trade Organization, 7, 45
Israel, 49, 50

Jackson, John H., 43–47, 60–63, 65
Japan, 12 n.3

Market access, 35, 54–55, 61, 62
Membership
  GATT, 9
  services agreement, 22
Monopoly policies, 29, 36
Most-favored-nation (MFN) principle, 60, 63
  "foot-dragger" problem, 11, 27, 46–47
  GATT provision, 8, 29, 32 n.4
  services agreement provision, 17, 20, 26–28, 35
Motion pictures, 64
Multinational corporations, 16

National Institute for Architectural Review Boards, 49
National security exception, 9, 29
National treatment obligation, 50, 55
  GATT provision, 8, 63
  implementation difficulties, 10, 15, 46, 47
  services agreement provison, 16, 17, 28–29, 35, 63–64
Nicaragua, 13–14 n.27

Optional protocol, 20, 54
  content and purpose, 17, 34–35, 60
  most-favored-nation principle, 17, 20, 35
  national treatment obligation, 17, 29, 35
  sector agreement relationship, 17, 35

Opt-out provision, 9, 29–30
Organization for Economic Cooperation and Development (OECD), 11 n.2, 45
Organization for Trade Cooperation, 21

Protocol of Provisional Application, 7, 9

Quotas, 8

Reciprocal Trade Agreements Act, 8
Reciprocity policy, 31, 53. *See also* National treatment obligation
Reed, John S., 41–42
Reporting requirements, 24–25, 29
Rivers, Richard R., 55–57, 61
Rostenkowski, Dan, 53

Secretariat, 17, 22, 55
Sector agreements (SSAs), 54
  content and purpose, 17, 35–36
  liberalizing criterion, 64
  optional protocol relationship, 17, 35
  umbrella code relationship, 18, 25–26, 35, 46
Semiconductor chips, 64–65
Services agreement. *See also* Optional protocol; Sector agreements; Umbrella agreement
  constitutional structure, 17–18, 45–46, 60
  development issues, 4–7, 54–55, 57–65
  GATT inapplicability, 15–16, 44–45
  national laws and regulations, relationship to, 18, 48, 58
  necessity for developing, 3, 37, 41–44, 55–57
  negotiators, 41, 42
  policy goals, 10–11, 48–53
Service trade
  comparative advantage, 4
  government regulation, 3–4, 43
  monitoring organizations, 11 n.2
  negotiating process, 53–54
  percentage of gross national product, 12 n.3
  U.S. trade surplus, 53
  what constitutes, 3, 12 n.4
Smith, Murray, 65
Snape, Richard, 63–64
South Korea, 12 n.5
Sovereignty concerns, 4–5
Spero, Joan, 57–59, 62
Subsidies, 8, 15, 16, 35, 64
Supervisory body, 17, 21–22, 25, 58
Switzerland, 51

Targeting strategies, 9
Tariff binding, 8
Telecommunications industry, 16, 49
Tokyo round, 45, 62
Tourism agreement, 50
Trade Act of 1974, 12 n.5
Trade agreements, 53. *See also* General
    Agreement on Tariffs and Trade;
    Services agreement
    United States–Canada free trade
        pact, 29, 49–50
    United States–Israel free trade pact,
        49, 50
    United States–United Kingdom
        bilateral services negotiation, 56
Trade surplus, 53
Transparency obligations, 24–25, 29, 35,
    46

Umbrella agreement, 20–33
    content and purpose, 17, 20, 46, 54,
        56
    dispute settlement, 23–24
    existing service agreements,
        relationship to, 31–32
    final clauses, 22, 31
    general exceptions, 29–30
    institutional measures, 21–22

measures for developing countries,
    30–31
most–favored–nation provisions, 26–
    28
national treatment obligation, 28–29
reciprocity, 31
regulatory due process, 25
sector agreements, relationship to,
    18, 25–26, 35, 46
statement of objectives, 20–21
transparency obligations, 24–25
waiver provisions, 30
United Kingdom, 12 n.3, 56
United Nations Conference on Trade and
    Development, 11 n.2
United States
    bilateral trade agreements, 29, 49–50,
        56, 64
    service trade, percentage of GDP, 12
        n.3
Uruguay round, 4, 41, 44

Voting structure, 21–22, 46, 62

Waiver provisions, 30
World Bank, 7, 18, 21
World Intellectual Property
    Organization, 11 n.2

A NOTE ON THE BOOK

This book was edited by Trudy Kaplan of the
publications staff of the American Enterprise Institute.
The index was prepared by Patricia Ruggiero.
The text was set in Palatino, a typeface designed by Hermann Zapf.
Coghill Book Typesetting Company, of Richmond, Virginia,
set the type, and Edwards Brothers Incorporated,
of Ann Arbor, Michigan, printed and bound the book,
using permanent, acid-free paper.